WORKFORCE 2000

Work and Workers for the Twenty-first Century

William B. Johnston
Project Director

Arnold H. Packer
Co-Project Director

With Contributions By
Matthew P. Jaffe
Marylin Chou
Philip Deluty
Maurice Ernst
Adrienne Kearney
Jane Newitt
David Reed
Ernest Schneider
John Thomas

HUDSON INSTITUTE
Indianapolis, Indiana

HI-3796-RR

June 1987

Published by Hudson Institute, Inc.
Herman Kahn Center
5395 Emerson Way
P.O. Box 26-919
Indianapolis, IN 46226 USA
Telephone: (317) 545-1000
Telex 855477

Printed in the United States of America.
Typeset, printed, and bound by Corporate Press Inc., Washington, D.C.

Ninth Printing November, 1990

This book may be ordered by

Writing to:
Hudson Institute
P.O. Box 26-919
Indianapolis, IN 46226

Library of Congress Catalog Card No. 87-601910

ISBN # 1-55813-004-7

ABOUT HUDSON INSTITUTE

Hudson Institute is a private, not-for-profit research organization with headquarters in Indianapolis, Indiana. Hudson specializes in the analysis of policy problems and the formulation of policy options for government and private sector clients. Hudson analysts strive to approach research in a creative and innovative fashion, while at the same time stressing the importance of providing decisionmakers with practical, usable analyses. Hudson's goal is to help policymakers make the best possible decisions within constraints of time, money, and information.

In its work, Hudson employs various methods and disciplines, but relies on no single specific methodology. This electic, multidisciplinary approach has become the hallmark of Hudson Institute studies. Hudson researchers were among the pioneers in the use of "scenarios" —a technique used to gain insights by posing alternative hypothetical future outcomes. Scenarios help to give decisionmakers a better understanding of the likely consequences of various policies, as well as the implications of both likely trends and less likely, but not implausible, events.

There are no "official" Hudson Institute positions. Hudson studies reflect the views of those who work on them. Hudson's staff includes about 35 research professionals experienced in many disciplines, but sharing a broad, multidisciplinary outlook. In addition to its full-time professional staff, the Institute has access to its public and fellow members, as well as to a wide range of expert consultants in the United States and abroad.

The Institute was founded in 1961 by the late Herman Kahn and colleagues from the Rand Corporation. Initially, the Institute's primary focus was on policy issues involving national security and international order. This emphasis reflected Herman Kahn's contributions to the understanding of nuclear strategy in his books *On Thermonuclear War, Thinking About the Unthinkable*, and *On Escalation*. The Institute's research has always emphasized the value of a long-term perspective on policy issues, and therefore the development of techniques for studying the future —especially the long-range future.

In 1984, Hudson moved its headquarters to Indianapolis, Indiana. Hudson also maintains offices in Alexandria, Virginia; Montreal, Canada; Brussels, Belgium; and Bonn, Federal Republic of Germany, and manages the Center for Naval Analyses in Alexandria, Virginia.

ACKNOWLEDGMENTS

Hudson Institute takes a broad multifaceted approach to futures research, relying on expertise from many disciplines. This project has been conducted in that tradition. Within the institute, many researchers made significant contributions to the study. Among the most important were those of Matthew Jaffe on the future skill requirements of the economy, Marylin Chou on the impacts of women and older workers on the economy, Philip Deluty on the shift to services, Adrienne Kearney on the impacts of immigration, Jane Newitt on the demographics of the future workforce, David Reed on economic scenarios, Ernest Schneider on future social and political changes, John Thomas on workplace literacy, and Maurice Ernst on the dynamics of the international economy. In addition, the project benefited from the ideas, criticism and advice of Frank Armbruster, Denis Doyle, Rob Melnick, and Jimmy Wheeler, the research assistance of Brad Huang and Nancy Bernardon, and the skillful editing of Carol Kahn and Ernest Schneider. Yvonne Swinton and Karen Whitehouse provided essential administrative support. Perhaps most importantly, the insight, patience, and support of Hudson's President Thomas D. Bell, Jr. contributed vitally to the project's success.

In addition, *Workforce 2000* has benefited from the counsel and criticism of a group of distinguished experts from outside Hudson Institute. Meeting periodically to review the research results, this group has been invaluable in testing the ideas, probing the evidence, and critiquing the logic of the study's recommendations. These experts included Gordon Berlin of the Ford Foundation, Pat Choate of TRW, William Kolberg of the National Alliance of Business, Malcolm Lovell of George Washington University, Connie Newman, and Robert Teeter of Robert Teeter Associates. Mac Lovell, in particular, contributed to the project, not only with his sharp insights, but with his gracious hospitality on numerous occasions. While these advisors bear no responsibility for the report's conclusions or its analysis, they

vi

have helped immensely in sharpening the research focus and clarifying the issues.

The research that led to this book was funded by a grant from the Employment and Training Administration of the U.S. Department of Labor. While the department deserves credit for its far-sighted commitment to long-range policy research, it bears no responsibility for the conclusions and policy recommendations presented here. The research, writing, analysis, and judgements of *Workforce 2000* were left exclusively to the study's authors, and do not necessarily reflect the views of the Department of Labor or any of its officials.

While they bear no blame for the failings of this study, three officials within the department deserve great credit for initiating and pursuing the *Workforce 2000* project. Secretary William E. Brock, whose concern with these issues preceded his leadership of the Department of Labor, provided the original inspiration for undertaking the work and valuable guidance as it progressed. Roger D. Semerad, Assistant Secretary for Employment and Training, and Roberts Jones, Deputy Assistant Secretary, have been invaluable supporters of the project from its inception. Without Roger's vision and boldness in undertaking this research, it could not have been started. And without Roberts' cooperation, support, and patience, it could not have been completed. As public officials entrusted with great responsibilities for the future welfare of the workforce, they deserve high praise for their courage and vision in support of this work.

William B. Johnston
Project Director

Arnold H. Packer
Co-Project Director

Indianapolis, Indiana
June 1987

ABOUT THE AUTHORS

William B. Johnston is a Senior Research Fellow at the Hudson Institute and President of Hudson Analytical Services, Inc., the corporate consulting arm of Hudson Institute. He is project director of Hudson's Workforce 2000 study. Before joining Hudson Institute, Mr. Johnston was director of public policy research for the Conference Board, a business research organization headquartered in New York. From 1979 to 1981, he was Assistant Secretary for Policy and International Affairs of the U.S. Department of Transportation. Prior to his service with the Department of Transportation, Mr. Johnston was Associate Director of the White House Policy Staff, where he specialized in transportation, international maritime policy, and economic development. He came to the White House from the George Washington University Center for Social Policy Studies, where he was a research fellow.

Mr. Johnston received his B.A. from Yale University in 1967 and studied economics and mathematics at George Washington University from 1972-1976. He is the author or co-author of a number of books including *Michigan Beyond 2000*, University Press of America, 1987; *Still a Dream, the Changing Status of Blacks Since 1960*, Harvard University Press, 1975; and *Work is Here to Stay, Alas*, Olympus Publishing Company, 1973. His articles have appeared in the *New York Times*, *The Washington Post*, *The Washington Star*, *Fortune*, and the *Monthly Labor Review*, among others.

Arnold H. Packer is a Senior Research Fellow at Hudson Institute and deputy director of the Work Force 2000 study. A former professional engineer, Dr. Packer came to Washington in 1969 as an economist for the Office of Management and Budget with responsibility for forecasting the U.S. economy. After working on energy policy for the Committee for Economic Development, he became the first chief economist for the newly-formed Committee on the Budget in the U.S. Senate. In 1977, he returned to the executive branch to become Assistant Secretary for Policy, Evaluation, and Research at the U.S. Department of Labor. In 1982, he formed Interactive Training, Inc., to produce interactive vidodisc training courses (SKILLPACS) to teach basic workplace skills.

Dr. Packer has written widely about economics, employment and training policies, and the use of technology for training, including a book, published by the MIT press, on computer-based models of the economy. He holds a Ph.D. in economics from the University of North Carolina at Chapel Hill. He also has a masters degree in business administration (from Sacramento State) and a bachelors degree in mechanical engineering (from the Brooklyn Polytechnic University).

TABLE OF CONTENTS

Acknowledgments v

About the Authors vii

List of Tables x

List of Figures.. xi

Executive Summary xiii

1. THE FORCES SHAPING THE AMERICAN ECONOMY 1

    The Integration of the World Economy...................................... 1

    The Shift of Production from Goods to Services 20

    The Proliferation of Advanced Technologies 32

    Renewed Productivity Growth, Particularly in Services................. 37

    Disinflation or Deflation in World Prices.................................. 43

    Increased Competition in Product, Service, and Labor Markets 48

2. SCENARIOS FOR THE YEAR 2000 51

    Three Projection of the Future.. 51

    The Surprise-Free Scenario: Outcomes and Impacts 57

    Alternative Scenarios.. 70

3. WORK AND WORKERS IN THE YEAR 2000............................. 75

    Demographics as Destiny—WORKFORCE 2000.......................... 75

    The Changing Job Mix.. 95

4. SIX CHALLENGES 105

    Stimulating World Growth.. 106

    Improving Productivity in Service Industries 107

    Improving the Dynamism of an Aging Workforce 110

    Reconciling the Needs of Women, Work, and Families................. 112

    Integrating Blacks and Hispanics Fully into the Workforce............ 114

    Improving Workers' Education and Skills.................................. 115

LIST OF TABLES

1	The U.S. Economy in the Year 2000	xvi
1-1	High-Earning Occupations Employ a Growing Share of the Workforce	31
1-2	But More Workers Are Earning Low Wages	31
2-1	The U.S. Economy in the Year 2000	54
2-2	Goods Production Will Shrink Further by the Year 2000	57
2-3	Employment in Goods Production Will Decline by the Year 2000	58
2-4	Most New Jobs Have Been Created by Small Firms	60
3-1	U.S. Population Growth, 1950–2000	76
3-2	The Labor Force is Growing Slowly	78
3-3	The Population Over Age 65 Will Grow More Slowly	80
3-4	Women Are a Growing Share of the Workforce	85
3-5	Non-Whites Are a Growing Share of the Workforce	89
3-6	Blacks and Hispanics Are Much Less Successful in the Labor Market	90
3-7	The Changing Occupational Structure, 1984—2000	97
3-8	The Occupations of the Future Will Require More Education	98
3-9	Fast-Growing Jobs Require More Language, Math, and Reasoning Skills	99
3-10	Black Men and Hispanics Face the Greatest Difficulties in the Emerging Job Market	102

LIST OF FIGURES

1   Low-Skilled Jobs are Declining xxii

2   Blacks and Hispanics Face the Greatest Difficulties in the
    Emerging Job Market xxiii

1-1   Exports and Imports Are a Growing Share of U.S. GNP 2

1-2   U.S. Growth Mirrors World Growth 5

1-3   The U.S. Trade Balance Declined Sharply After 1975 14

1-4   The Real Value of the Dollar Rose Rapidly During the
      Early 1980s 16

1-5   During the Early 1980s American Unit Labor Costs Rose Faster
      Than Those of West Germany or Japan 18

1-6   Services Are the Largest Share of Production in Advanced
      Industrial Countries 21

1-7   The Nine Largest U.S. Service Industries (1986) 22

1-8   Goods Production Is a Declining Share of Nominal GNP and
      Employment 24

1-9   Manufacturing's Share of the U.S. Economy in
      "Constant" Dollars 25

1-10 Production Workers' Wages are a Shrinking Share of
      Manufacturing Value 26

1-11 Production Workers' Wages are a Small and Declining Share of
      U.S. GNP 27

1-12 Service Industry Wages are Less Equally Distributed 30

1-13 The Cost-Effectiveness of Computers Continues to Rise
      Geometrically 33

1-14 Productivity Has Declined Substantially Since 1965 38

1-15 Low Productivity Growth in Services Has Slowed U.S.
      Economic Growth 39

1-16 Output Per Worker is Lower in Farming Than in the Rest
      of the Economy 40

1-17 Service Industries Lag Behind Manufacturing in Output
      Per Worker 41

1-18 OPEC Capacity Greatly Exceeds Production 44

1-19 The Prices of Agricultural Goods Have Been Declining............. 45

2-1 U.S. Productivity Rebounds, Offsetting Slower Labor Force Growth... 55

2-2 Service Industry Establishments Are Smaller.......................... 60

2-3 Services Moderate the Business Cycle.................................... 62

2-4 Productivity Gains in Services Are the Key to Future Economic Growth.. 65

3-1 Population and Labor Force Growth Will Drop by 2000............. 77

3-2 The U.S. Population Is Growing Older 80

3-3 The Middle-Aging of the Workforce 81

3-4 Young People Are More Likely to Move 83

3-5 Young People Are More Likely to Change Occupations............. 84

3-6 Women Hold a Growing Share of Managerial and Professional Jobs 86

3-7 Most New Entrants to the Labor Force Will Be Non-Whites, Women or Immigrants.. 95

3-8 Low-Skilled Jobs are Declining 100

WORKFORCE 2000
EXECUTIVE SUMMARY

The year 2000 will mark the end of what has been called the American century. Since 1900, the United States has become wealthy and powerful by exploiting the rapid changes taking place in technology, world trade, and the international political order. The last years of this century are certain to bring new developments in technology, international competition, demography, and other factors that will alter the nation's economic and social landscape. By the end of the next decade, the changes under way will produce an America that is in some ways unrecognizable from the one that existed only a few years ago.

Four key trends will shape the the last years of the twentieth century:

- *The American economy should grow at relatively healthy pace*, boosted by a rebound in U.S. exports, renewed productivity growth, and a strong world economy.

- Despite its international comeback, *U.S. manufacturing will be a much smaller share of the economy in the year 2000* than it is today. Service industries will create all of the new jobs, and most of the new wealth, over the next 13 years.

- *The workforce will grow slowly, becoming older, more female, and more disadvantaged.* Only 15 percent of the net new entrants to the labor force over the next 13 years will be native white males, compared to 47 percent in that category today.

- *The new jobs in service industries will demand much higher skill levels* than the jobs of today. Very few new jobs will be created for those who cannot read, follow directions, and use mathematics. Ironically, the demographic trends in the workforce, coupled with the higher skill requirements of the economy, will lead to both higher and lower unemployment: more joblessness among the least-skilled and less among the most educationally advantaged.

These trends raise a number of important policy issues. If the United States is to continue to prosper—if the year 2000 is to mark the end of the *first* American century—policymakers must find ways to:

- *Stimulate Balanced World Growth*: To grow rapidly, the U.S. must pay less attention to its share of world trade and more to the growth of the economies of the other nations of the world, including those nations in Europe, Latin America, and Asia with whom the U.S. competes.

- *Accelerate Productivity Increases in Service Industries*: Prosperity will depend much more on how fast output per worker increases in health care, education, retailing, government, and other services than on gains in manufacturing.

- *Maintain the Dynamism of an Aging Workforce:* As the average age of American workers climbs toward 40, the nation must insure that its workforce and its institutions do not lose their adaptability and willingness to learn.

- *Reconcile the Conflicting Needs of Women, Work, and Families:* Three-fifths of all women over age 16 will be at work in the year 2000. Yet most current policies and institutions covering pay, fringe benefits, time away from work, pensions, welfare, and other issues were designed for a society in which men worked and women stayed home.

- *Integrate Black and Hispanic Workers Fully into the Economy:* The shrinking numbers of young people, the rapid pace of industrial change, and the ever-rising skill requirements of the emerging economy make the task of fully utilizing minority workers particularly urgent between now and 2000. Both cultural changes and education and training investments will be needed to create real equal employment opportunity.

- *Improve the Educational Preparation of All Workers:* As the economy grows more complex and more dependent on human capital, the standards set by the American education system must be raised.

The U.S. Economy in the Year 2000

Because long-range forecasts are so uncertain, alternative scenarios are useful to help to bracket a range of possible outcomes. The three scenarios presented here are based not only on different rates of economic growth, but on different policy choices.

The baseline or "surprise-free" scenario reflects a modest improvement in the rate of growth that the nation experienced between 1970 and 1985. But despite improved trends in inflation and productivity, the U.S. economy does not return to the boom times of the

1950s and 1960s. Slow labor force growth is only partly offset by faster productivity gains, and imperfect coordination between the world's governments leads to only moderate rates of world growth. Economic turbulence causes periodic recessions in the U.S. that hold total growth to just under three percent per year.

In contrast, "world deflation" focuses on the possibility that a worldwide glut of labor and production capacity in food, minerals, and manufactured products could lead to a sustained price deflation and sluggish economic growth. World governments, chastened by a decade and a half of inflation, are slow to recognize the new economic realities and unwilling to undertake coordinated efforts to respond to them. The U.S., whose huge trade deficit has been the world's growth engine during the early 1980s, moves toward balance in its trade and fiscal accounts. Without U.S. stimulus, the rest of the world slides into a series of recessions that lead to increased protectionism and beggar-thy-neighbor trade, monetary, and fiscal policies that hold growth to only 1.6 percent per year over the period.

The third scenario, the "technology boom," outlines a powerful rebound in U.S. economic growth to levels that compare with the first two decades following World War II. Coordinated international monetary, fiscal, and trade policies succeed in smoothing world business cycles. Renewed public and private lending to developing nations and low oil prices trigger rapid growth in much of the Third World. In the U.S., high rates of investment in both physical and human capital, coupled with rapid productivity growth in services, low inflation, low resource prices, lower taxes, and less government intervention combine to produce a boom in productivity that causes the U.S. economy to surge ahead by 4 percent per year.

Table 1 summarizes the major assumptions and outcomes of the three scenarios. The table underscores several key points about the U.S. economy over the next 13 years:

● *U.S. Growth and World Growth are Tightly Linked:* The strong historical correlation between world growth and U.S. growth continues through the balance of the century. In the baseline forecast, the U.S. grows at about 2.9 percent, compared to 3.1 percent for the world.

Table 1
THE U.S. ECONOMY IN THE YEAR 2000

	1985 Level	BASE		2000 (Three Scenarios) LOW		HIGH	
		Level	Change*	Level	Change*	Level	Change*
World GDP (bill. 82$)............	7745	12204	3.1%	9546	1.4%	13057	3.5%
U.S. GNP (bill. 82$)...........	3570	5463	2.9%	4537	1.6%	6431	4.0%
GNP Deflator (1982-100)............	111.7	182.4	3.3%	117.8	0.4%	196.4	3.8%
Employment (millions)............	107.2	131.0	1.3%	122.4	0.9%	139.9	1.8%
Manufacturing............	19.3	17.2	-0.8%	18.0	-0.4%	18.1	-0.4%
Commercial & Other Services .	62.0	84.3	2.1%	76.5	1.4%	88.7	2.4%
Productivity (output/worker,82$).	33.3	41.7	1.5%	37.1	0.7%	46.0	2.2%
Manufacturing............	40.4	71.4	3.9%	58.0	2.5%	81.3	4.8%
Commercial & Other Services .	29.9	34.1	0.9%	30.4	0.1%	38.2	1.6%
Fed. Surplus (bill. curr.$)	-200.8	-110.0	—	-170.1	—	-40.7	—
Curr. Acct. Bal. (bill. curr.$)	-116.8	14.0	—	12.5	—	32.6	—
Disp. Income Per Capita							
(thou. 82$)	10.5	13.5	1.7%	11.5	0.6%	15.6	2.7%

*Average Annual Gain
Source: Hudson Institute.

• *U.S. Manufacturing Employment Declines While Services Grow:* Despite strong export growth and substantial production increases, manufacturing jobs decline in all scenarios. Whether the U.S. and world economies are booming in an open trading environment or growing slowly in an atmosphere of protectionism and nationalistic trading patterns, U.S. manufacturing jobs decrease. No pattern of growth enables manufacturing employment to return to the peak of 1979.

In addition to the decline in employment, manufacturing will decline as a share of GNP, measured in current dollars. Where manufacturing produced some 30 percent of all goods and services in 1955, and 21 percent in 1985, its share will drop to less than 17 percent by 2000.

The shift to services will bring with it broad changes in the location, hours, and structure of work. Service jobs tend to be located where and when the customer wants them, rather than centralized as are manufacturing jobs. Partly as a result, the typical workplace in the future will have fewer people, and the average workweek will become shorter with more people employed part-time.

The shift to services will also have great impacts on the economy and its employees. For example, the business cycle should moderate, since service industry growth is less volatile than manufacturing. Wages may become less equally distributed, since service jobs tend have more high and low earners, and fewer in the middle. Economic growth may be harder to achieve, because productivity gains are lower in most service industries.

Most importantly, the shift to services means that efforts to preserve or develop the nation's manufacturing base are swimming upstream against a powerful tide. Productivity gains, not Japanese competition, will gradually eliminate manufacturing jobs. Lower prices (relative to services) will gradually shrink manufacturing's share of the economy. Just as agriculture lost its central role in the American economy at the beginning of the century, so will manufacturing lose economic importance as the century draws to a close. Those who fail to recognize these inevitable trends—for example, states that try to capture new factories to boost their local economies or the Congress, which is threatening to legislate trade barriers to hang on to U.S. manufacturing jobs—will miss the most important opportunities of the future.

• *The Key to Domestic Economic Growth is a Rebound in Productivity, Particularly in Services:* Throughout the 1970s and early 1980s, the United States managed to sustain a rising standard of living by increasing the number of people at work and by borrowing from abroad and from the future. These props under the nation's consumption will reach their limits before the end of the century: there will be relatively fewer young people and homemakers who will enter the workforce during the 1990s, and the burden of consumer, government, and international debt cannot be expanded indefinitely. If the U.S. economy is to grow at its historic 3 percent per year average, the nation must substantially increase its productivity.

Output per worker during the 1990s is projected to double, from 0.7 percent per year to 1.5 percent, the same rate as the 1960s. A combination of older, more stable, and better-educated workers, and higher rates of investment will support this improvement. Better productivity performance by the service industries will be particularly important. Output per worker in manufacturing continues to show strong gains, but the most important productivity improvements come in services, where output per worker climbs from -0.2 percent over the last 15 years to +0.9 percent per year from 1985 to 2000. The keys to such advances will be more competition in traditionally noncompetitive industries such as education, health care, and government services, coupled with the application of advanced technologies to deliver more automated business, government, and personal services.

• *U.S. Trade Accounts Move Toward Balance:* Although the different scenarios show widely dispersed rates of growth of imports and exports, the U.S. current account balance improves under all conditions. This is due both to the devaluation of the dollar that has already taken place against other currencies and to improving productivity in manufacturing industries. Under the baseline scenario, by the year 2000 the U.S. current account balance is in the black by some $14 billion.

• *The U.S. Budget Deficit Declines:* Along with the improvement in the trade deficit comes a decline in the budget deficit. Even without any major tax increases, growth in GNP and a large surplus in the Social Security Trust Fund cut the federal budget deficit to $18 billion by 1995.

• *Inflation Moderates:* Under the baseline scenario, prices increase by an average of 3.3 percent per year over the 1985–2000 period. The excess world capacity in labor, goods, and services prevents inflation from resuming its pace of the 1970s.

● *Unemployment Remains Stubbornly High:* The baseline scenario forecasts unemployment at just over 7 percent in the year 2000, despite the relatively slow growth of the labor force projected over the period. In the deflation scenario, unemployment climbs above 9 percent, while even in the boom scenario unemployment is reduced only to 5.9 percent.

● *Disposable Income Increases Moderately:* Disposable personal income per person, the best single measure of how rapidly society is improving its standard of living, grows by 1.7 percent per year under the baseline scenario, almost precisely the rate at which it grew between 1970 and 1985.

Workers and Jobs in the Year 2000

Changes in the economy will be matched by changes in the workforce and the jobs it will perform. Five demographic facts will be most important:

● *The population and the workforce will grow more slowly than at any time since the 1930s:* Population growth, which was climbing at almost 1.9 percent per year in the 1950s, will slump to only 0.7 percent per year by 2000; the labor force, which exploded by 2.9 percent per year in the 1970s, will be expanding by only 1 percent annually in the 1990s. These slow growth rates will tend to slow down the nation's economic expansion and will shift the economy more toward income-sensitive products and services (e.g., luxury goods and convenience services). It may also tighten labor markets and force employers to use more capital-intensive production systems.

● *The average age of the population and the workforce will rise, and the pool of young workers entering the labor market will shrink:* As the baby boom ages, and the baby bust enters the workforce, the average age of the workforce will climb from 36 today to 39 by the year 2000. The number of young workers age 16–24 will drop by almost 2 million, or 8 percent. This decline in young people in the labor force will have both positive and negative impacts. On the one hand, the older workforce will be more experienced, stable, and reliable. The reverse side of this stability will be a lower level of adaptability. Older workers, for example, are less likely to move, to change occupations, or to undertake retraining than younger ones. Companies that have grown by adding large numbers of flexible, lower-paid young workers will find such workers in short supply in the 1990s.

- *More women will enter the workforce:* Almost two-thirds of the new entrants into the workforce between now and the year 2000 will be women, and 61 percent of all women of working age are expected to have jobs by the year 2000. Women will still be concentrated in jobs that pay less than men's jobs, but they will be rapidly entering many higher-paying professional and technical fields. In response to the continued feminization of work, the convenience industries will boom, with "instant" products and "delivered-to-the-door" service becoming common throughout the economy. Demands for day care and for more time off from work for pregnancy leave and child-rearing duties will certainly increase, as will interest in part-time, flexible, and stay-at-home jobs.

- *Minorities will be a larger share of new entrants into the labor force:* Non-whites will make up 29 percent of the new entrants into the labor force between now and the year 2000, twice their current share of the workforce. Although this large share of a more slowly growing workforce might be expected to improve the opportunities for these workers, the concentration of blacks in declining central cities and slowly growing occupations makes this sanguine outlook doubtful.

- *Immigrants will represent the largest share of the increase in the population and the workforce since the first World War:* Even with the new immigration law, approximately 600,000 legal and illegal immigrants are projected to enter the United States annually throughout the balance of the century. Two-thirds or more of immigrants of working age are likely to join the labor force. In the South and West where these workers are concentrated, they are likely to reshape local economies dramatically, promoting faster economic growth and labor surpluses.

In combination, these demographic changes will mean that the new workers entering the workforce between now and the year 2000 will be much different from those who people it today. Non-whites, women, and immigrants will make up more than five-sixths of the net additions to the workforce between now and the year 2000, though they make up only about half of it today:

	1985 Labor Force	Net New Workers, 1985–2000
Total	115,461,000	25,000,000
Native White Men	47%	15%
Native White Women	36%	42%
Native Non-white Men	5%	7%
Native Non-white Women	5%	13%
Immigrant Men	4%	13%
Immigrant Women	3%	9%

Source: Hudson Institute.

Juxtaposed with these changes in the composition of the workforce will be rapid changes in the nature of the job market. The fastest-growing jobs will be in professional, technical, and sales fields requiring the highest education and skill levels. Of the fastest-growing job categories, all but one, service occupations, require more than the median level of education for all jobs. Of those growing more slowly than average, not one requires more than the median education.

Ranking jobs according to skills, rather than education, illustrates the rising requirements even more dramatically. When jobs are given numerical ratings according to the math, language, and reasoning skills they require, only twenty-seven percent of all new jobs fall into the lowest two skill categories, while 40 percent of current jobs require these limited skills. By contrast, 41 percent of new jobs are in the three highest skill groups, compared to only 24 percent of current jobs (see Figure 1).The changes ahead in the job market will affect different groups in the society in different ways. While young whites may find their jobs prospects improving, for black men and Hispanics the job market will be particularly difficult (see Figure 2). In contrast to their rising share of the new entrants into the labor force, black men will hold a declining fraction of all jobs if they simply retain existing shares of various occupations. Black women, on the other hand, will hold a rising fraction of all jobs, but this increase will be less than needed to offset their growing share of the workforce.

Six Policy Challenges

These trends in the emerging economy suggest six policy issues that deserve the greatest attention:

Stimulating World Growth: For more than a decade, American policymakers have been concerned with the U.S. balance of trade, the nation's deteriorating ability to compete with other nations, and the

Figure 1
LOW SKILLED JOBS ARE DECLINING

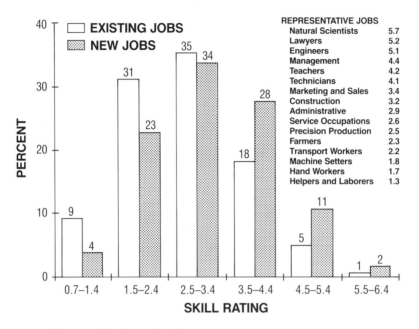

Source: Hudson Institute.

presumed unfairness of the trading policies of other countries. These issues, while important, are not the most critical international concerns facing the nation. U.S. prosperity between now and the end of the century will depend primarily on how fast the world economy grows and on how rapidly domestic productivity increases. It will depend very little on how open or closed the Japanese market is to American goods, or even on how soon U.S. trade accounts return to balance.

In particular, it is important for the United States, along with other industrial countries, to find ways to restimulate growth in the developing world. These nations that are still on the threshold of industrialization have the greatest opportunities for rapid growth that can stimulate the world and U.S. economies.

At the same time, efforts to improve U.S. competitiveness must always be undertaken within the context of strengthening the world economy. The envy and anger that many in the United States feel toward Japan's success should not blind policymakers to the reality

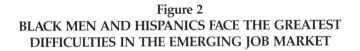

Figure 2
BLACK MEN AND HISPANICS FACE THE GREATEST
DIFFICULTIES IN THE EMERGING JOB MARKET

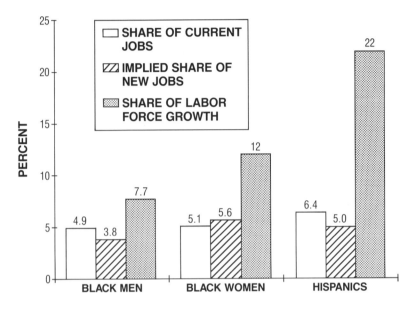

that as Japan (and every other nation of the world) grows richer, the
United States will benefit. Just as it is easier for a company to prosper
in a rapidly-growing market than to capture market share in a
shrinking one, so it will be easier for the United States to prosper in
rapidly-growing world markets than in static or shrinking ones.

Of course, the U.S. *share* of world growth is also important. But
most of the steps that must be taken taken to improve U.S. competitiveness have little to do with changing the behavior of the Japanese
or the Koreans. Instead, they involve changes in the propensity of
Americans to borrow and spend rather than to save, major improvements in the educational preparation of large numbers of prospective
workers, and reforms in the practices and laws that encourage
America's best and brightest to provide legal advice in corporate
takeovers rather than to build companies that exploit new technologies.

Improving Productivity in Service Industries: Manufacturing still
controls the imagination, the statistics, and the policies of the nation,
even though it now represents a small and shrinking fraction of

national employment and output. The nation's mental image of progress continues to be one in which manufacturing plants produce more cars, computers, and carpets per hour. But services are a far larger segment of the economy and the sector whose productivity has actually declined in recent years. These industries—health, education, trade, finance, insurance, real estate, and government—must be the targets of government efforts to improve productivity.

To realize this objective, new efforts must be made to tear down the barriers to competition in many of the service industries where competition does not now exist. At the same time, new investments must be made in research and development targeted toward improving service industry productivity.

In education, for example, competition is needed at the elementary and secondary school level, where the monopoly position of the public schools has stifled innovation. In order to provide a benchmark for measuring gains, national standards and nationally comparable tests are essential. At the same time, new investments are needed in educational technology, in particular to develop a large base of public domain software to teach math, reading, science, and more advanced courses.

In health care, the steps taken to inject competition into the system must be extended, while new investments are made in productivity-enhancing technologies such as automated diagnostics. In a range of other government services, privatization and competition promise to provide great productivity gains.

Improving the Dynamism of an Aging Workforce: At the same time that the workforce is aging and becoming less willing to relocate, retrain, or change occupations, the economy is demanding more flexibility and dynamism. Despite general recognition of the importance of a flexible workforce, many national policies fail to promote this end.

For example, the nation's pension system is one in which most retirement benefits are tied to the job. In many cases, employees receive no benefits if they leave after a few years, and, by the time they reach mid-career, they would suffer major benefit losses if they switched employers. The current system tends to inhibit workers from changing jobs and to discourage companies from hiring older workers.

Similarly, the unemployment insurance system has been largely used to provide income support to workers who are laid off. Relatively little has been done to make the system one that promotes relocation, retraining, and job search.

Although worker retraining has become a catchphrase, and the federal government and private industry now spend billions of dollars for retraining, there is still no national consensus that all workers should expect to learn new skills over the course of their worklives. Except in a few companies, training is confined mostly to the top and bottom ranks of employees, with little systematic effort to insure that all workers are constantly reinvesting in themselves to avoid obsolescence. National policies that promote such corporate and individual attitudes toward retraining should be backed up with changes in the tax code to encourage lifelong education.

Finally, the goal of promoting dynamism requires reconsideration of national policies on immigration. The most careful studies of legal immigrants have concluded that they are a valuable asset to the nation and help to stimulate economic growth and change. The need for more, better-educated immigrants to help staff a growing economy will increase as the growth of the population and labor force slows in the 1990s. Despite the political and social objections, the nation should begin a program of gradually increasing its quotas and opening its doors to more individuals desiring to enter the country.

Reconciling the Demands of Women, Work, and Families: America has become a society in which everyone is expected to work—including women with young children. But many of society's institutions were designed during an era of male breadwinners and female homemakers.

What is needed is a thoroughgoing reform of the institutions and policies that govern the workplace, to insure that women can participate fully in the economy, and that men and women have the time and resources needed to invest in their children. For example, some formula is needed to provide parents with more time away from work. Flexible hours, the use of sick leave to care for children, more part-time work, pregnancy leaves for mothers and fathers, and other innovations are expensive, but ultimately necessary changes in the structure of work that will accommodate the combination of work and family life. Similarly, the need for high-quality day care has not yet been fully addressed. Government and private mechanisms to provide for the care of the children of working parents need further development.

The increase in the numbers of working women also has implications for the current debate over welfare reform. The current stay-at-home welfare program was designed long before most women worked. Now that a majority of nonwelfare women with young children work, it no longer seems cruel to require welfare mothers to do so. The current system should be replaced with one that mandates work for all able-bodied mothers (except for those caring for infants), while providing training, day care, and job counseling.

Integrating Blacks and Hispanics Fully into the Workforce: For minority workers, the changes in the nation's demography and economy during the 1990s represent both a great risk and a great opportunity. With fewer new young workers entering the workforce, employers will be hungry for qualified people and more willing to offer jobs and training to those they have traditionally ignored. At the same time, however, the types of jobs being created by the economy will demand much higher levels of skill than the jobs that exist today. Minority workers are not only less likely to have had satisfactory schooling and on-the-job training, they may have language, attitude, and cultural problems that prevent them from taking advantage of the jobs that will exist.

If the policies and employment patterns of the present continue, it is likely that the demographic opportunity of the 1990s will be missed and that by the year 2000 the problems of minority unemployment, crime, and dependency will be worse than they are today. Without substantial adjustments, blacks and Hispanics will have a smaller fraction of the jobs of the year 2000 than they have today, while their share of those seeking work will have risen.

Each year of delay in seriously and successfully attacking this problem makes it more difficult. Not only will the jobs become more sophisticated and demanding, but the numbers of new workers entering the workforce will begin to increase after 1993. Now is the time to begin investing in education, training, and other assistance. These investments will be needed, not only to insure that employers have a qualified workforce in the years after 2000, but to finally deliver the equality of opportunity that has been America's great unfulfilled promise.

Improving Workers' Education and Skills: As the economies of developed nations move further into the post-industrial era, human capital plays an ever-more-important role in their progress. As the society becomes more complex, the amount of education and knowledge needed to make a productive contribution to the economy becomes greater. A century ago, a high school education was thought to be superfluous for factory workers and a college degree was the mark of an academic or a lawyer. Between now and the year 2000, for the first time in history, a majority of all new jobs will require postsecondary education.

Education and training are the primary systems by which the human capital of a nation is preserved and increased. The speed and efficiency with which these education systems transmit knowledge governs the rate at which human capital can be developed. Even more than such closely-watched indicators as the rate of investment in plant and equipment, human capital formation plays a direct role in how fast the economy can grow.

If the economy is to grow rapidly and American companies are to reassert their world leadership, the educational standards that have been established in the nation's schools must be raised dramatically. Put simply, students must go to school longer, study more, and pass more difficult tests covering more advanced subject matter. There is no excuse for vocational programs that "warehouse" students who perform poorly in academic subjects or for diplomas that register nothing more than years of school attendance. From an economic standpoint, higher standards in the schools are the equivalent of competitiveness internationally.

Promoting world growth, boosting service industry productivity, stimulating a more flexible workforce, providing for the needs of working families with children, bringing minority workers into the workforce, and raising educational standards are not the only items on the nation's agenda between now and the year 2000. But they are certainly among the most important.

More critically, they are issues that will not go away by themselves. If nothing unusual is done to focus national attention and action on these challenges, they are likely to be still unresolved at the beginning of the next century. By addressing them now, the nation's decisionmakers can help to assure that the economy and the workforce fulfil their potential to make the year 2000 the beginning of the next American century.

CHAPTER 1

The Forces Shaping The American Economy

How will the U.S. economy develop in the future? Between now and the year 2000, a number of powerful economic forces will reshape American jobs and industries. The most important trends will be:

- Continued Integration of the World Economy
- Further Shifts of Production from Goods to Services
- The Application of Advanced Technologies to Most Industries
- Faster Gains in Productivity, Particularly in Services
- Disinflation or Deflation in World Prices
- Increased Competition in Product, Service, and Labor Markets

In varying degrees, the patterns that will shape the future are visible in recent economic history. A brief review of the past sheds light on how these forces will act on the economy and interact with each other between 1987 and 2000:

The Integration of the World Economy

Gradual improvements in transportation and communications technologies have slowly woven the world's economic fabric more tightly together. Railroads and long-haul trucks, coupled with radio and television broadcasting and microwave telecommunications, created a national U.S. market during the first six decades of this century. Since the 1960s, container ships, jet airplanes, and satellite and fiber optic communications have created an international one. Even the lowest value products now travel around the globe from producers to consumers: logs cut in the forests of Vancouver travel to Japan to become lumber and then return across the Pacific to become houses in Southern California. World markets establish the prices, not

Figure 1-1
EXPORTS AND IMPORTS ARE A
GROWING SHARE OF U.S. GNP

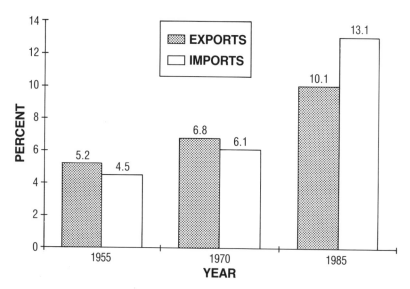

Source: Wharton Econometrics, Inc.

only of such commodities as wheat, coal, and oil, but of manufactured goods such as clothing, automobiles, and semiconductors.

The shrinking time and distance that separate countries and continents have caused world trade in goods and services to rise much faster than world gross domestic product (GDP). Traded goods and services now account for a larger fraction of world GDP than ever before. Between 1973 and 1984, GDP in the industrial market economies grew at an average of 2.4 percent annually, while merchandise trade grew at 4.2 percent annually. Between 1965 and 1983, exports climbed from 12 to 18 percent of GDP in the developed countries.

The United States has shared in this rapid growth of global trade. Between 1955 and 1985, for example, the export share of GNP almost doubled, while the import share nearly tripled (see Figure 1-1).

More recently, both capital and labor markets have also become globally integrated. Only a decade ago, borrowing foreign currencies or investing in foreign assets was restricted to the most sophisticated multinational companies. Today, individual Americans routinely buy mutual funds investing in the Japanese stock market, and Japanese investors pour billions of dollars into American real estate and the U.S. Treasury bond market.

Labor, which the economist Adam Smith characterized as immobile, now flows around the world with increasing ease. Where formerly a few managers and technicians crossed international borders for overseas jobs, now whole armies of workers travel from Turkey to labor in German factories, from Korea to build Saudi Arabian petrochemical plants, or from Mexico to staff American restaurants.

The Loss of Economic Sovereignty

As the world economy has become more integrated, the United States, like all other nations, has progressively lost control of its economic destiny. The growing importance of trade means that no nation can expect sustained growth unless the world economy also grows. These parallel growth patterns are reinforced by the tight linkages between national fiscal and monetary policies. The U.S. can no longer unilaterally set its own interest rates, balance its trade accounts, or finance its deficit without consideration of the policies and attitudes of other countries. A vast network of currency traders, central banks, and corporations determines relative currency valuations, trade flows, and national interest rates. These, in turn, influence rates of economic growth, sectoral shifts, unemployment rates, and other national economic outcomes. Sovereignty over economic matters has become a shared power.

Although economic integration has been under way for many years, its impacts have only become decisive in the U.S. within the last two decades. During the 1970s, the OPEC oil shocks and worldwide patterns of inflation and recession forced U.S. decision-makers to recognize the reality of global interdependence. The cutoff of imported oil served to underscore this new reality. Just as national defense had become a multilateral undertaking, so U.S. economic growth had become inextricably intertwined with world growth.

The loss of control over the domestic economy was much more difficult for U.S. policymakers to recognize and accept than it was for other nations. Japan, West Germany, and other countries never controlled more than a small fraction of world trade, even though they devoted a substantial fraction of their GNPs to trade. These nations were accustomed to planning economic policies in light of international economic conditions that were beyond their control.

In contrast, during the early postwar era, the United States dominated world trade, even though it devoted only a small part of its GNP to exports. As a result, the U.S. largely ignored international conditions in planning its economic policies. American economic forecasters typically devoted a few minutes to speculating about trade issues, after carefully analyzing domestic housing starts, the U.S. savings rate, and Detroit's auto sales.

In 1960, for example, the U.S. devoted less than 6 percent of GNP to exports, but controlled a fifth of world trade. American companies dominated international commerce, the American dollar was the international medium of exchange, and American technology was unrivaled. So omnipotent did American multinationals seem during the 1960s, that the conventional wisdom—enshrined in *The American Challenge* by a French author, J. Servan-Schreiber—was that Europe was at risk of being swallowed by U.S. cultural and economic power.

By the mid-1980s, Servan-Schreiber's awe of American power had become a quaint historical footnote, as the U.S. position in world trade eroded. In 1984, the U.S. devoted more than 10 percent of its GNP to exports, but its share of world exports had dropped below 9 percent. Although the U.S. position had simply become more like that of other nations, American economic decisionmakers were shocked by the loss of control that resulted from the erosion of U.S. economic preeminence. Now the Federal Reserve must consider the attitudes of Japanese and German bankers before deciding on a discount rate. Mortgage rates rise or fall, depending less on American personal savings than on the strength of the dollar against the yen. Union and management negotiators in Detroit must review wage patterns in Seoul and Tokyo before signing new contracts. Economic forecasters are forced to study the West German discount rate, Latin American debt, and OPEC oil prices before estimating American growth. Just as state economic strategists in New York or California are required to begin their planning with an understanding of the direction of the U.S. economy, so the possibilities for U.S. economic growth are constrained by economic patterns around the world.

Seen from this perspective, the path of the U.S. economy over the next 13 years will depend substantially on events and decisions elsewhere in the world. The rate at which the world economy grows and the competitive actions of other nations will be as important as

Figure 1-2
U.S. GROWTH MIRRORS WORLD GROWTH
(Moving Average of Three Previous Years)

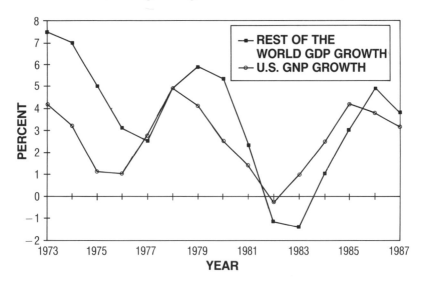

Source: Wharton Econometrics, Inc.

actions taken in the U.S. Without rapid world growth in both developed and developing nations, the U.S. cannot hope to sustain strong growth at home. And unless American productivity rises more rapidly than that of its principal competitors, domestic economic growth will lag behind other nations.

Globalization and U.S. Future Economic Growth

Over the past 25 years, the U.S. economy has closely mirrored the world economy. With few exceptions, in years in which the world has been booming, the United States has been booming; when the world has been in recession, so too has the United States (see Figure 1-2).

The reason for this tight linkage is straightforward: as trade grows in importance, it accounts for more of U.S. growth. When Japan expands rapidly, it buys more Boeing jets for Japan Airlines, uses more American medical instruments in Japanese hospitals, and sends more wealthy Japanese tourists to visit the United States. Just as rapid growth in California's Silicon Valley created jobs in Michigan auto plants and New York investment banks, so growth in Japan and Korea has created jobs in San Francisco hotels and Seattle aircraft plants. The market for U.S. goods and services has grown to include not only the 50 states, but also the 178 countries of the world.

Although U.S. growth has closely paralleled world growth over the past two and a half decades, it has not equalled it. Between 1960 and 1985, the world economy grew at an average rate of 3.9 percent per year, while U.S. growth averaged 3.1 percent annually. As a result of this slower growth, the U.S. share of the world economy (including eastern bloc nations) dropped from 35 percent in 1960 to 28 percent in 1985.

It is likely that this pattern of similar, but slower, U.S. growth compared to the world economy will continue in the years ahead. As a mature industrial economy, the United States is unlikely to be able to match the pace of productivity gains and economic growth that will be experienced by countries that are still in the early stages of industrialization. Over the next 13 years, growth in the developing world should resume its rapid pace, fueled by large gains in the size of the labor force, the continuing shift from subsistence agriculture to manufacturing, and rising educational levels. On the other hand, moderate productivity gains and slow labor force growth in the service-dominated U.S. economy mean that it will be quite difficult for the U.S. to match world growth rates and that the U.S. share of the world economy will fall further by the year 2000.

As obvious and unremarkable as these observations may be, they have been widely ignored in recent debates concerning the nation's economic future. Much discussion of competitiveness, trade balances, and other measures has focused exclusively on the U.S. position relative to the rest of the world and failed to recognize the overwhelming interest the nation has in the economic success of other nations. The real challenge for the United States is to increase its own productivity, while stimulating maximum world growth—not to capture economic activity from other nations.

Put simply, the Japanese, the Germans, the Koreans, and the Brazilians are not stealing American jobs—they are creating them. Just as Korea or Brazil profit from strong growth in Europe and North America, so the United States gains from growth in Asia and Latin America. More important than the competition among nations for high-productivity industries and good jobs is the collective effort to maximize world growth. The world is not a zero-sum game in which the U.S. must level the playing field in order to win a fair share of jobs. Instead, U.S. self-interest dictates that it stimulate the economies of other nations, since this is the most important way of creating American jobs.

In particular, the extraordinary attention that has been directed toward the competition between the United States and Japan has been misplaced. The United States has been one of the greatest beneficiaries of the huge advances in productivity and economic growth that Japan has enjoyed during the postwar era. Not only are the cars, television sets, and VCRs purchased by Americans cheaper and of higher quality than they would otherwise be, the total size of the U.S. economy and the number of U.S. jobs are certainly greater because of Japan's success, rather than despite it. If Japan were somehow returned to the small, low-productivity economy that existed after World War II, American citizens would suffer nearly as much as the Japanese.

Conversely, each step that is taken to restrict our trade with Japan—from holding down auto imports to forcing the Japanese to raise the prices of computer chips—will cause the U.S. to grow more slowly that it would without such restrictions. Not only will the prices of U.S. goods rise, making U.S. consumers effectively poorer, but the size of U.S. markets will shrink as Japanese economic growth slows. Even without a tit-for-tat trade war, restrictions on Japanese imports will certainly harm the U.S. economy.

These observations about Japan apply as well to America's other trading partners. Far from being alarmed by the strong growth of South Korea and Taiwan, or concerned about West Germany's large trading surplus, the United States should recognize that the success of these nations is working to help promote world growth and development, stimulating demand for American products, and helping to boost the American economy.

In the years ahead, these lessons will be extended to other nations, as the circle of U.S. trading partners and competitors expands. By the year 2000, the U.S. will be benefiting from much expanded trade with China, India, and Latin America, just as it earlier gained from trade with Canada, Europe, Japan, South Korea and Taiwan.

The problem for America is not the healthy saving, investment, and productivity of other countries, but the weakness of these factors in the U.S. economy. Individuals, communities, regions, and countries that continuously spend beyond their means, fail to invest wisely, or ignore opportunities to increase their productivity will not be as prosperous as those that do. The solutions lie with changes in domestic U.S. economic performance, not with attempts to balance trading accounts or protect U.S. industries.

Stimulating World Economic Growth

The integration of the world economy will be easier if the world grows rapidly. With hundreds of millions of new workers flooding into the cities of the developing world, growth rates of 5–6 percent annually would be required to utilize fully the world's productive capacity and prevent the army of the unemployed from growing. This is far higher than current forecasts, which mostly contemplate 3–4 percent growth.

Whether even these forecasts will be reached will depend mostly on the amount of fiscal and monetary stimulus that is collectively applied to the world economy by national governments. In particular, the policies of Japan, West Germany, and other large OECD economies will play a central role. Unless those nations pursue much more stimulative policies, there is considerable likelihood that the world, and the U.S., will grow sluggishly over the next decade and a half.

Throughout the early 1980s, the U.S. was the world's fiscal engine of growth, using huge budget deficits to stimulate world demand and absorb exports. This unilateral Keynesianism cannot be sustained during the late 1980s and 1990s. Although concern over the budget deficit may not translate into spending cuts, political pressures will reduce the rate of growth of U.S. spending. For the next few years, large new domestic spending initiatives are unlikely, and real defense spending is likely to be flat. Revenues, on the other hand, should rise steadily, both because of economic growth and, possibly, tax increases. The combination of higher revenues and flat spending will gradually reduce the federal deficit.

During the late 1980s and 1990s, this pattern of deficit reduction is likely to be reinforced by growing surpluses in the Social Security Trust Funds. For example, between 1984 and 1988, the difference between revenues and expenditures in the basic Social Security and Medicare programs shifted from − $26 billion to + $15 billion. During the 1990s, these positive annual balances will continue to rise, helping further to trim the deficit.

At the same time, the traditional fiscal surpluses of state and local governments will continue. Between 1970 and 1985, for example, state and local governments collected about 1.1 percent more of GNP in taxes than they spent. During the 1990s, the states will continue to be net savers, as they emphasize pay-as-you-go financing and set aside funds to support future employee pensions.

These anticipated increases in government savings are needed to bring U.S. consumption and investment back into balance with U.S. production and to reduce the U.S. trade deficit. But if the U.S. is not to continue to absorb the world's excess production capacity, the responsibility for stimulating the world economy will shift to Japan, West Germany, and other industrial nations. Many of these nations are extremely reluctant to boost demand through either monetary or fiscal policies. After more than a decade of relentless inflation, central bank authorities in West Germany and Japan have been cautious about expanding their money supplies and wary of pushing the growth of their economies above historic averages. If inflation remains under control through the late 1980s, these attitudes may become less pervasive, leading to greater willingness to stimulate world demand. In the near-term, however, it is likely that lower U.S. deficits will not be fully offset by greater stimulus from other nations, and world demand growth will be sluggish as a result. Current forecasts by the IMF and others suggest that the world will not achieve even 3 percent growth during the late 1980s, much less the 5–6 percent growth of the 1960s.

Rebalancing World Growth

Almost as important as the gross level of stimulus will be the correction of severe imbalances in the current world economy. In order to maximize world growth, the distortions in world financial markets that have been created by inflation and unsound government investment policies must be corrected. The world's financial institutions must rechannel capital from the rich, aging nations of the world to the young, industrializing countries where real rates of return are likely to be higher. To accomplish this, the United States must cease consuming so much of the world's savings, by reducing its massive trade and budget deficits.

Managing the Inflation Cycle

The imbalances that have developed over the past 15 years can be traced in large measure to the powerful cycle, first of high and accelerating inflation, followed by severe disinflation. As the countries of the world scrambled to shield themselves from the huge increases in the cost of oil during the 1970s, they triggered great instabilities in the real values of their various currencies, which sent a series of false signals to the world economy.

Because inflation fluctuated so widely among countries and over time during these years, it made calculations of real rates of return much more uncertain than usual. This was particularly true for projects with long-term payoffs. A corporate planner trying to decide whether to construct a plant in Mexico or Brazil discovered that assumptions about relative trends in inflation and exchange rates dwarfed the importance of fundamental calculations about the current costs of labor, materials, and land. As a result, many unsound projects were financed, and many more worthwhile investments were delayed or abandoned, because planners could not properly calculate their potential returns. The fact that inflation resulted in low, or even negative, rates of return in the industrial countries during the late 1970s encouraged many banks to seek more risky loans at higher nominal yields, while borrowers, particularly in the Third World and in natural resource industries, plunged into debt, expecting to be able to repay in depreciated currencies. Between 1970 and 1984, for example, the total external public debt of the developing countries grew from $69 billion to $828 billion, or from 13 percent to 34 percent of their combined GNPs.

The sharp turn toward monetary restraint in the United States in 1980 triggered a severe recession, a lasting decline in commodity prices, and a sharp increase in real interest rates. This disinflation cycle exposed the unsoundness of the debts that had been incurred by many of the LDCs and others dependent on natural resource prices. Although the world has weathered the early years of the process of unwinding from this massive debt overhang without triggering a banking crisis, the process has led to a new set of imbalances. As lenders have reversed direction and attempted to improve the quality of their portfolios in a new, lower inflation environment, they have retreated from higher-risk lending of all kinds, particularly to many LDCs.

This flight from LDC lending threatens to undermine world economic growth, because these nations offer the greatest prospects for rapid economic gains. A combination of demographic, structural, and educational factors makes the developing world a place where investments offer particularly high real rates of return. Many developing nations are converting their economies from agrarian to industrial modes, with huge gains in productivity and production. For example, among the middle income LDCs, agriculture's share of production dropped from 21 to 14 percent between 1965 and 1984, while industry grew from 31 to 37 percent. Educational levels are also rising rapidly in many developing countries, further increasing the potential for rapid industrial progress. Among the middle income countries, the proportion of teenagers in high school climbed from 20 percent to 47 percent over the 1965–1983 time period. As a result of these favorable economic conditions, abetted by the huge lending from the rich nations, the developing nations have grown much more rapidly than the OECD countries in recent years. Between 1970 and 1984, the GNP of the developing countries grew by 95 percent in real terms, while that of the developed countries rose only 60 percent.

If the world can achieve some sustained measure of monetary stability over the next few years, the false signals sent to the world economy by inflation/deflation may fade away. As inflation subsides, the fundamental returns to investment should again begin to guide world capital markets, leading to a renewal of lending and faster growth in the less developed nations of the world.

Improving Government Allocation Decisions

Along with the distortions caused by world inflation have been great imbalances created and sustained by governments. If new lending is to produce solid real investment returns, the unsound investment decisions of many governments will require reform. The need for changes extends from the richest and most developed nations such as the United States to the poorest developing nations.

During the past 15 years, there have been two major new accumulations of world capital. The first was caused by the sharp increase in oil prices during the 1970s, which by 1983 had concentrated some $380 billion in the hands of the OPEC nations. The second resulted from the huge savings and spectacular trading surpluses accumulated by Japan during the 1980s. According to one study, Japan will control $700 billion in overseas assets by the end of the 1980s.

The world's financial institutions in which these resources were deposited chose to recycle them in large part in loans to nations rather than to enterprises. The size of the surpluses, the difficulties in understanding complex local economic conditions, and the presumed safety of government loans all contributed to this pattern. For the most part, however, governments were not wise investors of these resources. Much of the OPEC surplus was used to finance unproductive investment and consumption in the developing world. Some of these funds were used to finance oil imports, while many other loans underwrote the construction of redundant steel, auto, and petrochemical plants in various LDCs. Within the OPEC nations, much of the wealth was used to support higher levels of consumption and investments in dubious schemes for industrial development.

More recently, large Japanese trade surpluses have been directed back into U.S. Treasury securities, in effect underwriting the American budget deficit. By continuing to run massive deficits, the U.S. government absorbed a huge share of net new world savings. But rather than directing these resources toward productive U.S. investments, the government simply allowed them to be spent by American consumers.

In both cases, capital resources accumulated in one part of the world were used for consumption or for unproductive investment in others. Importantly, it was the unsound decisions of governments, rather than unwise investments by industrialists, that dissipated the capital. In aggregate, the world's productivity gains were undermined by these large capital surpluses that world governments failed to recycle into productive investments.

In combination, the slower growth policies pursued by many developed countries in the wake of the years of high inflation, coupled with the failure to allocate resources around the world in an efficient manner, contributed substantially to the poor performance of the world's economy after 1973. Between now and the year 2000, the most important prerequisite to strong U.S. growth will be a reversal of this pattern: stable policies of fiscal and monetary stimulus coordinated among Japan, West Germany, the U.S., and other developed nations; renewed lending to the underdeveloped nations, particularly in Latin America; sounder investment policies in the developing world; and a reduction in the U.S. budget deficit.

Improving American Competitiveness

Even with robust world growth, the United States cannot expect to enjoy a rapidly rising standard of living unless it maintains a strong competitive position in world trade. Yet for all the attention that national competitiveness has received, there is little agreement concerning the definition of the term, the roots of the problem, or the steps that should be taken to insure U.S. competitiveness.

A basic definition of competitiveness is simply the ability of domestic producers to sell sufficient goods and services outside the country to pay for American imports. It is not enough, however, merely to sell abroad or to match the price of imports. Exports must be able to support wages and profits that are better than those the nation has historically enjoyed. For competitiveness to be a sensible national objective, it cannot simply be purchased at the price of a lower standard of living. From this perspective, competitiveness is really another way of looking at national productivity. The emphasis should not be on balancing import and export ledgers, but on increasing national wealth through productivity gains.

In general, international trade has almost always worked to promote increased productivity and wealth in the United States. Throughout the postwar era, higher levels of exports and imports have been accompanied by a rising U.S. standard of living. Of course, some industries, regions, and companies have not gained from trade but have suffered lower sales, lower wages, and lower profits as a result of competition from abroad. But on a national basis, the losers from trade have been far outnumbered by the gainers. The well-known benefits of comparative advantage and specialization have meant that, on a national basis, increases in imports and exports have never been purchased at a cost of lower real wages or profits.

The recent imbalances in American trade accounts, particularly vis-a-vis Japan, have led many to question this historic calculus of the benefits of trade. Over the past decade, the erosion of the competitive position of steel, automobiles, textiles, consumer electronics, and other U.S. manufacturing industries has led to widespread doubts concerning American industrial strength and a growing crescendo of support for trade restrictions.

Why did so many American industries lose their international competitiveness? Is the damage irrevocable or will it be corrected?

The Roots of America's Competitive Problem

Until about 1970, the U.S. balance of trade remained slightly positive (see Figure 1-3). In 1971, merchandise trade flows dipped

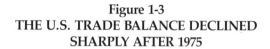

Figure 1-3
THE U.S. TRADE BALANCE DECLINED
SHARPLY AFTER 1975

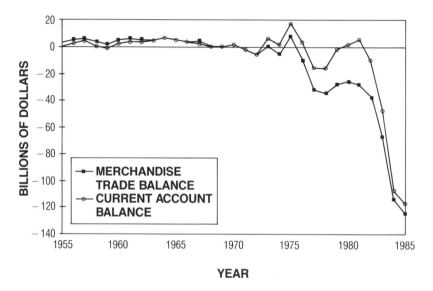

YEAR

Source: Economic Report of the President, 1987

into the red for the first time since World War II, but large surpluses in the service accounts—principally profits from foreign investments—kept overall trade flows balanced. After recovering somewhat in the mid-1970s, merchandise trade turned sharply negative in 1976 and continued to grow steadily worse over the next decade, reaching −$65 billion in 1983 and −$140 billion in 1986. By 1982, the gap in merchandise trade was large enough to make the overall U.S. balance of trade negative, and, by 1986, this overall deficit had plunged to −$144 billion. The reasons for this record can be traced to four related events:

• *Gradual Loss of the American Productivity Advantage:* Throughout the postwar era, U.S. manufacturing productivity has been growing more slowly than that of its chief trading partners and competitors. Between 1950 and 1983, for example, output per hour of U.S. workers increased by 129 percent. Canadian workers' productivity rose by 215 percent during the same period; the war-ravaged economies of

France and West Germany increased output per hour by 458 and 508 percent. Japanese workers increased their output per hour by a staggering 1,624 percent.

Importantly, the faster gains of America's trading partners were primarily the result of the broad diffusion of advanced manufacturing systems throughout the world. Other nations, who entered the 1950s with vastly inferior infrastructure, capital plant, equipment, knowledge, and technologies gradually acquired the resources they needed to bring their manufacturing capabilities up to the world standard set by the United States.

But though other nations were rapidly gaining ground, the United States manufacturers remained superior in absolute terms throughout the 1960s in most industries. By the late 1970s, however, Japanese and West German productivity had so improved that the absolute productivity levels of some of their manufacturing industries had caught up with, and, in some cases, had surpassed American industries. In automobiles, for example, several studies in the late 1970s showed that Japanese carmakers could produce an automobile with 10–30 percent fewer hours of labor than American firms. Once Japanese firms had overtaken American manufacturers in absolute levels of productivity, the relatively slower productivity growth of American firms in the late 1970s began seriously to undermine American competitiveness. Between 1975 and 1980, output per hour in U.S. manufacturing rose by an average of 1.7 percent per year, compared to 3.8 percent in West Germany and 8.6 percent in Japan.

One factor that exacerbated the situation in some industries was the loss of volume that occurred as imports gained market share. For example, U.S. steel production dropped by more than one-fourth between 1975 and 1983, and the U.S. share of world steel production declined from 16 percent to 12 percent; for autos, the drop in volume was 22 percent, as the U.S. share of world production fell from 27 to 17 percent. Since these declines in volume and market share could not be fully offset by employment declines, overall labor productivity dropped.

● *Exchange Rate Fluctuations:* The pattern of exchange rate fluctuation over the 1970s and early 1980s exacerbated the effects of these relatively slower productivity gains. Currency realignments of 1971–72 and the sharp further depreciation of the dollar in 1978 and 1979 temporarily masked the unfavorable trend in U.S. competitiveness,

Figure 1-4
THE REAL VALUE OF THE DOLLAR ROSE
RAPIDLY DURING THE EARLY 1980'S

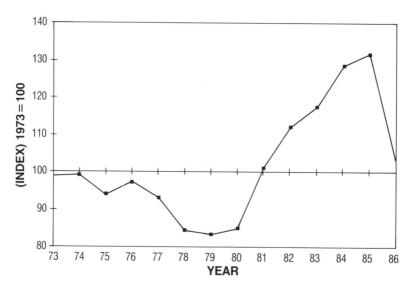

Source: Economic Report of the President, 1987

enabling the U.S. to maintain its share of manufactured exports and roughly to balance its current accounts. Between 1973 and 1979, for example, the real (inflation-adjusted) value of the U.S. currency dropped by 16 percent relative to the currencies of its major trading partners (see Figure 1-4).

This drop in the value of the dollar made imports more expensive and exports cheaper. It effectively disguised the decline in competitiveness that was occurring, enabling U.S. manufacturers to continue competing, even though their productivity and labor costs were not keeping pace with their competitors. When the dollar changed direction in late 1980, based on higher U.S. interest rates, greater confidence in U.S. economic prospects, and declining confidence in foreign economies, the weakness that had been building was suddenly revealed. By 1985, when the real value of the dollar had climbed almost 60 percent above its 1979 low, American manufacturers were in an untenable position. As exports slowed and imports boomed, U.S. producers scrambled to respond to unfavorable exchange rates, by moving production overseas and importing components and finished products from foreign plants. The spectacular deterioration in the U.S. trade balance that occurred in 1985 and 1986 was the result of the cumulative effect of exchange rates that effectively whipsawed U.S. industry—first shielding it from competitive realities and then overexposing it to foreign competition.

Higher Labor Costs: Slow relative growth in U.S. productivity was exacerbated during the late 1970s, as the country adjusted to the effects of rising oil prices. Because of differences in bargaining power, market conditions, and other factors, American manufacturing workers' wages rose faster than those of other workers during this inflationary period. In 1973, for example, U.S. manufacturing workers earned an average of 4 percent more than all U.S. workers; by 1980, the gap had widened to 9 percent. In effect, U.S. manufacturing workers bore less of the immediate burden of paying for the higher cost of oil. Their rising relative wages contributed to the erosion in the cost-competitiveness of American industry. The combination of higher wages and slow productivity growth caused U.S. unit labor costs to rise more rapidly than those of several foreign competitors during the late 1970s and early 1980s. Between 1973 and 1983, for example, unit labor costs rose at an annual rate of 7 percent per year in the U.S., compared to 4.4 percent in West Germany and 2.8 percent in Japan (see Figure 1-5).

• *The Emergence of Stronger Competitors:* While part of the decline in U.S. competitiveness can be explained in terms of lower productivity, higher wages, and fluctuating exchange rates, some of the explanation lies outside these macroeconomic variables. In the simplest terms, the competition became much tougher during the 1970s. In the 1960s, there were only a handful of companies outside the U.S. that could rival the enormous wealth of engineering, marketing, and manufacturing talent fielded by U.S. multinationals such as GM, Ford, GE, Westinghouse, and IBM. By the 1980s, the American giants had been joined by a number of companies that had become their technological and marketing equals. Toyota, Hitachi, Siemens, Phillips, Matsushita, and many others were capable of research, investment, and marketing on an equal footing with any competitor in the world.

Particularly in consumer products, where quality, reputation, and marketing are often as important as price, the new competitors have proven formidable. The story of the loss of American competitive strength is at least partly a story of superior products that have won market share, whether or not they were cheaper than American alternatives.

Japanese cars, for example, initially penetrated the U.S. market because they cost less than American models. During the 1960s, when the Japanese share of the U.S. market was climbing from 7 to 15

Figure 1-5
**DURING THE EARLY 1980's AMERICAN
UNIT LABOR COSTS ROSE FASTER THAN
THOSE OF WEST GERMANY OR JAPAN**

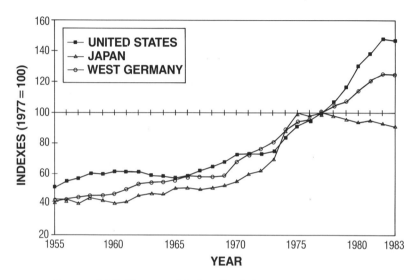

Source: U.S. Bureau of Labor Statistics

percent, the average Japanese car sold for about two-thirds as much as the average American model. By 1979, however, the average selling prices of Japanese cars had nearly equalled American prices, yet the Japanese share had risen to 22 percent. And by 1983, when Japanese cars cost *more* than American models, their share of the market had soared to 26 percent. Evidently, Japanese automakers had convinced consumers that their products were better than those made in Detroit. American competitors continued to lose market share during the 1980s, not because their higher cost structure had resulted in higher prices, but because they were making inferior products that could not compete even when they were sold more cheaply than imports.

Can American Manufacturers Compete?

How will the factors that have shaped U.S. competitiveness in recent years affect American manufacturers in the future? What are the prospects for a resurgence of American export strength?

A review of the likely trends indicates that American industry is poised for a remarkable recovery. While the competition from abroad has certainly not slackened, all of the basic macroeconomic factors—manufacturing productivity, unit labor costs, and exchange rate alignment—have shifted in favor of American competitors. During the late 1980s, American manufacturing exports are likely to expand strongly, while import gains level off.

Since the depths of the 1981 recession, U.S. manufacturing productivity has rebounded strongly. From the third quarter of 1981 to the third quarter of 1986, for example, U.S. manufacturing productivity grew at a 3.8 percent annual rate, far above the 1.5 percent rate that had prevailed between 1973 and 1981, and well above the postwar trend rate of 2.6 percent.

U.S. labor costs have also improved markedly. Strong productivity gains coupled with moderate wage hikes significantly improved the competitive position of U.S. workers. From 1982 to 1985, U.S. unit labor costs declined by 3 percent, compared with an increase of 2 percent for the wages of workers in the plants of America's major foreign competitors.

Until 1985, these relative improvements in productivity and unit labor costs were swamped by the growing strength of the U.S. dollar. But since its peak in the first quarter of 1985, the dollar has fallen by 31 percent against a trade-weighted average of major U.S. trading partners, standing now roughly where it was in 1973 before its first sharp decline. With the dollar now much more favorably aligned, the prospects for a revival of U.S. manufacturers are much improved.

Two obstacles remain that could slow or block this revival. First, the dollar has not fallen relative to the currencies of Canada and several developing countries whose products have begun to enter the U.S. market in substantial volumes. South Korea, Taiwan, Brazil, and Mexico have markedly improved their competitive positions during the early 1980s, and unless their currencies are revalued, they are likely to show substantial trade surpluses with the U.S. over the next few years.

Second, the competitive advantages that many Japanese and West German companies have built up in the American market may erode only slowly, even in the face of unfavorable macroeconomic conditions. In automobiles, for example, the voluntary restraint agreement between the United States and Japan has certainly held

Japanese car imports far below the levels they would have attained otherwise. Despite higher prices, American consumers are much more eager to purchase Japanese cars than market shares indicate. Thus, it may take much more drastic increases in the value of the yen and the price of Japanese cars before Japanese auto imports decline. Similarly, in some products such as consumer electronics, there is no serious American competition remaining to benefit from the U.S. dollar revaluation. Here also it may be many years before imports decline or U.S. competitors emerge.

Despite these uncertainties, the tremendous improvement in the economic fundamentals for American competitors suggests that U.S. export industries will rebound strongly in the future. By the year 2000, U.S. industry is likely to show new competitive vigor in international trade, and, as a result, U.S. merchandise trade accounts may be in balance or even surplus.

The Shift of Production from Goods to Services

The improvement in the U.S. trade balance will provide some stimulus to the nation's economy over the next 13 years. But, despite the increasing international competitiveness of American manufacturing firms, manufacturing is unlikely to be a major contributor to the growth of U.S. GNP or employment over the next decade and a half. Manufacturing, along with other goods production, is a small and shrinking share of the economy, and this share is sure to shrink further in the years ahead. The revitalization of American manufacturing will be a favorable development, but it will be much less important to U.S. economic prospects than changes in productivity and employment patterns in the service industries that dominate the U.S. economy.

Economic development follows a predictable pattern in which agricultural production shifts to manufacturing and then to services. While there have been variations in this pattern, the shift to services is so pervasive that it is a reliable barometer of the stage of industrial advancement that a country has achieved. In 1984, for example, low income countries devoted more than a third of their economies to agriculture, but only 30 percent to the production of services. Among the advanced industrial countries, the agricultural share accounted

Figure 1-6
SERVICES ARE THE LARGEST SHARE OF PRODUCTION IN ADVANCED INDUSTRIAL COUNTRIES
(1984)

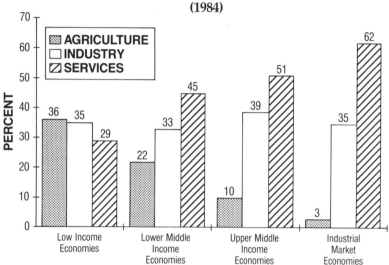

Source: The World Bank, World Development Report, 1986

for only 3 percent, while services comprised more than three-fifths of production. Middle income countries fell in between these levels (see Figure 1-6).

Despite the long history of this trend, and the pervasiveness of the phenomenon, the structural shift toward service industries is still poorly understood and often misinterpreted. What are service industries? How and why is the American economy continuing to shift to these kinds of economic activities? What will the shift mean for American employment, productivity, and wealth over the next 13 years?

What Are Service Industries?

Service industries differ from manufacturing, agriculture, and other goods-producing industries in that they create economic value without creating a tangible product. Some services, such as transportation and retailing, add value to manufactured goods by making them more available or useful to consumers. Others, such as education and health care, create value that is largely independent of the goods-producing economy. In addition, services usually create value at or close

Figure 1-7
THE NINE LARGEST SERVICE INDUSTRIES
(1986)

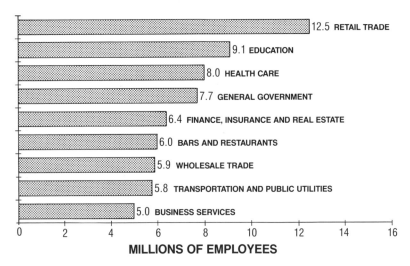

MILLIONS OF EMPLOYEES

Source: Derived from U.S. Bureau of Labor Statistics, *Employment and Earnings*, January, 1987

to the consumer, in both space and time. A few services (for example, finance) can be transported and stored—but most cannot be. For this reason, they are more difficult to trade internationally than goods.

Services are often stereotyped as low-productivity, low-wage industries such as fast food and barber shops. The reality is that many of the largest service industries involve relatively high wages and advanced technology. Although the largest single category is retail trade, education and health care are the second and third largest employers, followed by government and the finance industry (see Figure 1-7).

This list of service industries suggests that many commonly-held assumptions concerning the post-industrial economy are suspect. For example, the huge numbers of sales clerks, hospital orderlies, waiters, and truck drivers employed by service industries belie the use of the term "the information economy" as a synonym for services. Not all service industries are intensive users of information. On the other hand, the presence of such capital- and technology-intensive industries as medical care, finance, and transportation casts doubt on glib generalizations about the low quality of service jobs. Many service industries require extensive knowledge and training, and pay premium wages.

Measurement problems also cloud understanding of the shift to services. For example, the same economic activities may show up as manufacturing or as services, depending on the firm for which they are performed. When General Motors bought Electronic Data Systems, hundreds of EDS systems analysts who had been counted as service industry employees suddenly became manufacturing workers. As EDS staffers working in GM divisions, they had been allocated to services, because the establishment that employed them was primarily engaged in services. As employees in GM's EDS division, they worked for establishments that were primarily engaged in manufacturing.

While erroneous generalizations and measurement uncertainties may make the shift to services harder to understand, they do not make it any less important. Services will continue to reshape the U.S. economy over the next 13 years, affecting the rate of growth of the economy, the distribution of income, the location and organization of work, and the balance of U.S. trade.

The Changing Structure of the U.S. Economy

Much of the confusion over the scope and importance of the shift to services stems from a misunderstanding of how to measure and evaluate the restructuring that is occurring. Observers focusing on different measures of change can reach radically different conclusions. For example, when measured in terms of employment and nominal output, the goods share of the U.S. economy has been falling rapidly over the last 30 years. Many economists, however, focus on inflation-adjusted or "real" output as the best measure of underlying change. Using this index, goods production appears to be a stable share of U.S. GNP during the postwar era (see figure 1-8).

What do these different indexes mean? Which index is most relevant for predicting the future? Is the economy truly shifting to services or not?

Because almost all economic value in market economies is ultimately created by human labor (capital can be thought of as labor that can be stored and used later), the employment share is the best single measure of economic change. Over any significant period of time, employment shares will closely track actual economic activity and nominal output. In terms of understanding the future, the decline in employment shares and nominal output is far more important than the stability in "real" output. In fact, the "real" output

Figure 1-8
GOODS PRODUCTION IS A DECLINING
SHARE OF NOMINAL GNP AND EMPLOYMENT

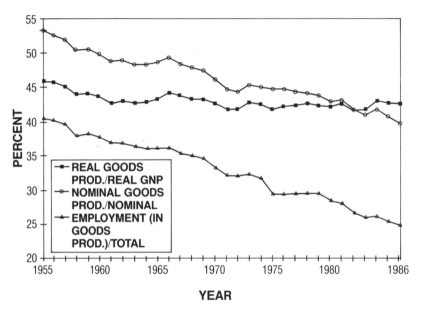

YEAR

Source: Economic Report of the President, 1987

measure is actually a purely hypothetical index. The actual activity in the economy—hours worked and dollars paid—is counted in the employment and nominal output totals.

The historical analogy of agriculture helps to clarify this point. Between 1947 and 1986, the value of farm output dropped from 8.6 to 1.6 percent of GNP, reflecting the shift of economic activity to the production of other goods and services, and the decline in farm prices relative to other goods. More efficient farms, bigger tractors, more fertilizer, hybrid seeds, and other advances meant that fewer workers and other resources were needed to feed the nation. If the 1986 economy were restated to reflect "real" 1947 prices, farming would represent 3.7 percent of GNP—more than twice as great a share as it actually holds. Although it might be comforting to economists to believe that farming is producing twice as much real wealth as the nominal figures record, this hypothetical money would be of little use to farmers.

Figure 1-9
MANUFACTURING'S SHARE OF THE U.S. ECONOMY IN "CONSTANT" DOLLARS

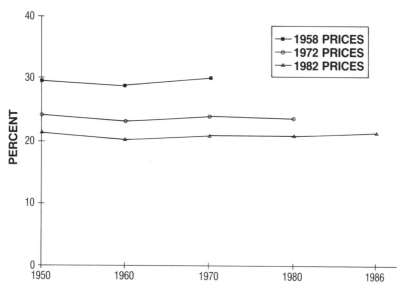

Source: Economic Report of the President, various years

A brief look at how manufacturing's "constant" share has been declining reinforces the point. Economists analyzing the economy during the Kennedy and Nixon years correctly noted that, in 1958 prices, the manufacturing share of "real" GNP was stable at about 30 percent. During the Carter years, a 1972 benchmark was used, and manufacturing was a stable 24 percent share of the "real" economy. The President's Economic Report in 1987 noted that manufacturing was maintaining a constant 21 percent share of U.S. GNP, measured in 1982 prices. Despite the often-observed record of stability, between 1958 and 1982, manufacturing had managed to decline from 30 to 21 percent of GNP, because manufacturing prices were rising more slowly than service industry prices. It was the "real" economy that was an illusion. The reality was a steadily shrinking manufacturing share of economic activity (see Figure 1-9).

Just as food production gradually shifted away from the farm into "upstream" industries (seed development, tractor production, and fertilizer manufacturing) and "downstream" industries (trucking, warehousing, food stores, and restaurants), manufacturing value is being increasingly created outside of the factory. To an ever-greater degree, the value of manufactured products is represented by services that occur upstream of the plant, such as product and market research, design, engineering, and tooling, or by downstream activities such as transportation, retailing, and advertising. Meanwhile, the factory itself is becoming ever more automated. As a result, its share of the total cost of production is dropping, and it is being rendered less and less important economically. During the postwar era, the share of total U.S. manufacturing value-added represented by the wages of production workers dropped from 40 to 24 percent (see Figure 1-10). Since manufacturing's share of the total economy

Figure 1-10
PRODUCTION WORKERS' WAGES ARE A SHRINKING SHARE OF MANUFACTURING VALUE

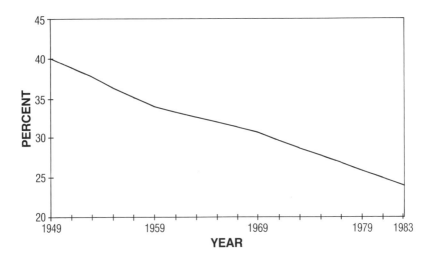

Source: Statistical Abstract of the U.S., 1986

was dropping over the same period, by 1983, the wages of production workers represented only 6.2 percent of U.S. GNP, down from 11.6 percent in 1949 (see Figure 1-11).

As manufacturing becomes more efficient, it requires fewer resources of all kinds—not only fewer people, but less capital and energy as well—to produce the same or greater quantities of goods.

Figure 1-11
PRODUCTION WORKERS' WAGES ARE A SMALL AND
DECLINING SHARE OF U.S. GNP

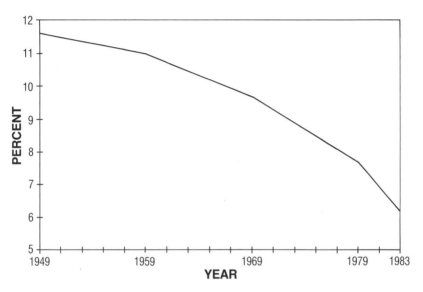

Source: Statistical Abstract of the U.S., 1986

Part of these productivity gains is passed on to consumers in the form
of lower (or more slowly rising) prices. It is these lower relative prices
for manufactured goods that are causing them to decline as a share of
nominal GNP, even though the volume of goods is rising. As this
transformation continues, manufacturing will become less and less
important to the economy as a mechanism for creating wealth.
Sometime during the next century, manufacturing may require as few
resources as today's agriculture. When this occurs, manufactured
goods will seem no more important to the nation's economy than
farm produce seems today. Manufactured goods, of course, will still
be produced in great quantities, just as huge amounts of food are
produced. But goods production will employ few people and generate a relatively small share of the nation's income.

Although the transformation away from agriculture now seems unremarkable, the shift away from manufacturing is still confusing and threatening to many. Just as during the fifteenth century the most learned French economists felt that farming was the only true source of wealth (and convinced Louis XI to use government money to create a domestic silk industry), so today there are those who see manufacturing as the only real creator of value and view services as somehow secondary or even parasitic. To these observers, for example, the so-called "hollowing" of U.S. industries as manufacturing plants move overseas is gravely alarming, since it seems further to undermine our ability to create wealth in this country.

Yet, understood in the context of the inevitable shift of economic activity toward services, the movement of plants overseas is not so much threatening as it is irrelevant. As manufacturing plants become less and less the places where economic value is created, their locations become less and less important. If only a handful of workers in highly automated plants is needed to make all the cars or cameras or compact disc players the world can buy, then the location of these plants becomes inconsequential.

It has been argued that, even if manufacturing represents only a small share of economic activity, the location of manufacturing plants still matters, because these facilities are the linchpins that control or direct the production of many auxiliary goods and services. If, for example, South Korea manufactures most of the world's steel, then presumably South Korean companies will ship most of the iron ore, South Korean engineers will design new steelmaking equipment, and South Korean accountants will balance the books.

But this analysis overestimates the impact of manufacturing geography on the location of other types of value-added. It is analogous to arguing that a strong French silkworm industry should have caused textile factories to locate in France or that Idaho potato farmers influence the locations of McDonald's restaurants. Increasingly, the upstream and downstream activities that contribute most of the value to manufactured goods take place far away from the location of production. Corporate headquarters can be moved at the whim of the chief executive. Research and development facilities can be sited in the woods of Vermont, along the southern coast of France, or wherever a supply of engineers and scientists can be hired. Accountants, consultants, lawyers, construction and tooling specialists, and many other service providers fly around the world to provide their talents to manufacturers, wherever they are located. Sales, marketing, and distribution, of course, occur chiefly in the country where the product is sold. The geography of plant locations is gradually losing its importance as determinant of where value is created in the goods economy.

Consider, for example, a major "American" product: personal computers sold by IBM. The components in these machines are manufactured in many locations around the world, including factories in Singapore, Taiwan, South Korea, and the USA. Because manufacturing represents less than 10 percent of the the selling price of the machine, the foreign share of the value created by IBM PC production is quite small. The majority of the value in these products is American, consisting of design, engineering, sales, and servicing, as well as the substantial overhead required to manage a large corporation. Far from threatening American economic growth, the IBM personal computer has been a tremendous boon to the nation, despite the offshore location of much of the manufacturing associated with the product.

In summary, the shift to services is the inevitable and healthy result of steady productivity gains occurring in manufacturing. Because productivity gains are easiest to achieve in the controlled, high-volume environment of the factory, the factory is becoming less and less important as a source of jobs; economic value is moving away from the plant into other activities. This process is not a threat to society's wealth-producing potential, it is a reflection of it; it represents a shift in the economic challenge to new sectors: retailing, health care, education, government, food service, and other industries. The nation's economic future will be written by these industries, not by the revival of manufacturing.

Are Service Jobs Good Jobs?

Suspicion of the service economy has been focused most recently on the quality of service employment. Service jobs, it has been alleged, are not only less productive than manufacturing employment, their earnings are less equally distributed. As a result, the shift to services is gradually eroding the middle class, creating a nation of haves and have-nots.

The most careful studies of the impact of the shift to services suggest that these concerns are largely unfounded. Although service industry wages are less equally distributed than those in manufacturing or government, the shift to services is not yet having a significant negative impact on the distribution of income. Instead, the slow growth of productivity in services, coupled with rapid increases in fringe benefits, has caused hourly compensation to grow slowly. The problem is not so much the inequality of service industry wages as it is the slow growth of those wages and their diversion to pay for pensions and medical bills.

When jobs are classified by industry, according to the shares in high- (more than $500 per week), middle-, and low-earning segments (less than $250), service industry wages are less equally distributed than those in goods production or government, and more workers are in the lowest-earning category. For example, in 1983, 40 percent of service industry workers earned less than $250 per week, compared to 30 percent of manufacturing workers, and only 22 percent of government workers (see Figure 1-12). But, despite this less equal distribution, the share of the workforce in the highest-earning third of

Figure 1-12
SERVICE INDUSTRY WAGES ARE LESS EQUALLY DISTRIBUTED

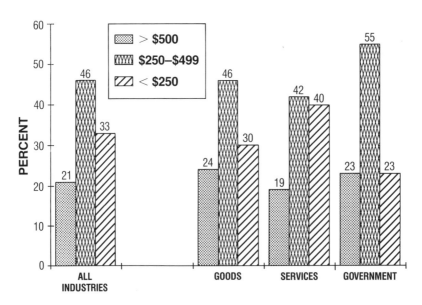

Source: Robert Z. Lawrence, *The Brookings Review*,
Fall 1984

Table 1-1
HIGH-EARNING OCCUPATIONS EMPLOY A GROWING
SHARE OF THE WORKFORCE
(percentages)

Distribution of Occupations (Standardized to 1982)	1973	1982
Top Third ($382–773 per week)	25.2	29.0
Middle Third ($264–382 per week)	34.2	32.5
Bottom Third ($71—264 per week)	40.6	38.5

Source: Patrick McMahon and John Tschetter, "The Declining Middle Class:
A Further Analysis," *Monthly Labor Review*, September, 1986, page 23.

occupations increased from 25 to 29 percent, while the share in the bottom third dropped from 41 to 39 percent between 1973 and 1982 (see Table 1-1).

When the workforce is analyzed according to weekly earnings rather than by occupation, the share of high-earning workers did decline during the late 1970s and early 1980s, as more junior, lower-paying positions were apparently created in all occupational groups (see Table 1-2). The share of the workforce in the lowest earning categories climbed by almost 4 percent between 1973 and 1985, with most of the shift coming from the decline in middle-wage jobs. But this shift toward the low end of the earnings spectrum was not the result of a hollowing of the middle class economy, as employment shifted to services. Rather it seems to have been a reflection of the higher numbers of young and female workers in the workforce in recent years and the generally slow growth of productivity in services. When productivity is growing fast, as it was during

Table 1-2
BUT MORE WORKERS ARE EARNING LOW WAGES
(percentages)

Distribution of Occupations (Standardized to 1982)	1973	1982
Top Third (>$385)	33.3	32.6
Middle Third ($239–385)	34.8	31.7
Bottom Third (<$239)	31.9	35.7

Source: Patrick McMahon and John Tschetter, "The Declining Middle Class:
A Further Analysis," *Monthly Labor Review*, September, 1986, page 25.

the 1960s, more of the new jobs will pay high wages; when it is growing slowly, as it has been recently, a greater fraction will pay poorly.

Even more important may have been the large increase in the share of wages devoted to fringe benefits in recent years. Between 1973 and 1985, fringe benefits (in 1985 dollars) rose by $150 billion, or 4 percent per year. Wages, on the other hand, rose by only 1.1 percent per year. Since most of these fringe benefits were part of the compensation of middle- and higher-earning workers, the rapid increase in fringe benefits appears to have accounted for a large share of the perceived decline in the share of high-wage jobs.

Slow productivity growth, coupled with the diversion of more of total compensation to Social Security, pensions, and health benefits, created the statistical illusion that fewer top-paying jobs were being created. In reality, the opposite was probably true: the economy has been creating more high-wage, high-skill jobs, not fewer.

The Proliferation of Advanced Technologies

Since the industrial revolution, technology has played a powerful role in reshaping the world's economy. During the early twentieth century, the rapid development or application of electricity, telephones, airplanes, and automobiles fundamentally restructured American cities and brought dramatic changes in the nature of work. At mid-century, the invention of computers, television, and jet aircraft brought more revolutionary change. During the last decade and a half of the century, the continued exploitation of these older technologies, along with the proliferating impact of new inventions, will bring important, and perhaps radical, transformations to the economy.

What will the most important technologies be? How will they be applied? How will they reshape the nation's jobs and industries?

In the relatively few years between now and the end of the century, the most important technologies are those that are already well-known and far along in their development. A few innovations that are still in the laboratory stage may be implemented by the year 2000, but the most important changes will flow from existing inventions. Five technologies will have the greatest impacts:

• *Information storage and processing:* The forty-year history of computing has been characterized by steady, apparently inexorable, improvements in the price/performance ratios of computing devices (see

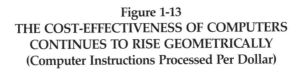

Figure 1-13
THE COST-EFFECTIVENESS OF COMPUTERS
CONTINUES TO RISE GEOMETRICALLY
(Computer Instructions Processed Per Dollar)

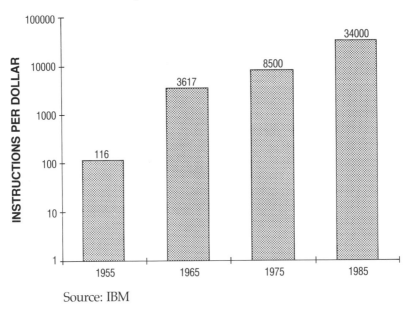

Source: IBM

Figure 1-13). Beginning in 1977, the industry entered a new phase in which the enormous power of very large-scale integrated circuits was coupled with the cost savings of a mass personal computer market. Today, many desktop microcomputers are more powerful than the machines that were used to guide the Apollo rocket that carried a man to the moon in 1968.

By the year 2000, microcomputers will be as powerful as today's mainframes. Today's memory chips that can store 256,000 or a million bits of information will have given way to chips with 10–30 times more storage capability. Today's microprocessors that can process one or two million instructions per second will have been succeeded by chips that are an order of magnitude more capable. Desktop storage will not be measured in today's megabytes (million words) but in gigabytes (billion words) and terabytes (trillion words). Machines that can analyze many different types of information at once, and enormously sophisticated software, will have finally resolved traditional debates over whether computers can ever really think like people. Artificial intelligence will be real.

In practical terms, this continuing evolution of computers will mean that it will be trivially cheap to apply staggering amounts of machine intelligence to jobs that are currently handled by people. Silicon secretaries that can take dictation and edit letters, reservation clerks that understand speech in any language, or robots that can load a truck or pick strawberries are easily within the reach of technologies being developed now. By the year 2000, such machines will be coming into wide use. Even much more sophisticated tasks, such as diagnosing illness or writing computer programs, may be partly automated by the turn of the century.

Communications: Along with the advances in computers will be parallel improvements in the country's communications systems. By the year 2000, the nation will be blanketed by a digital telecommunications network that will connect most businesses and many homes with fiber optic links of enormous capacity. Most homes will have some sort of home terminal (in addition to a traditional telephone) for accessing this system. This network will make realities out of current dreams such as home shopping and banking, working from the home, and even dial-up music or video entertainment. As more and more information is stored electronically and transmitted electronically, print media will begin to lose their historic advantage. The postal service and the newspaper industry (whose demise has been predicted for decades) will still be in existence, but the growth industries will be electronic communications. At the same time, new software industries will spring up to integrate, analyze, and present the huge array of electronic information that will be available. The providers of dial-up data will be both large companies and cottage collectors.

Advanced Materials: Many traditional materials used in industry will be replaced by much more sophisticated and useful synthetics. In particular, coatings of unprecedented hardness and durability will enormously extend the lives of moving parts and surfaces exposed to wear, weather, and extreme conditions. Diamond coatings, ceramics, and reinforced plastics will greatly increase the toughness, resilience, and useful life of many manufactured products. This improvement in the durability of durable goods, coupled with a continued trend toward less material-intensive products (and the shift to the service economy), will substantially reduce the use of raw materials. Jobs in durable goods industries, and those in industries whose output is sold by the ton, will decline.

Biotechnologies: The understanding of biological processes, and the ability to manipulate life forms at the cellular and sub-cellular level, have exploded in the last decade. The first fruits of the biotechnology revolution are already visible in world agriculture, where new plant varieties have been invented that can withstand extremes of temperature, moisture, and soil conditions, create their own fertilizer, or combine the best features of widely different strains. Super-producing milk cows, pigs that grow faster with less feed (and have less cholesterol), and chickens that are naturally resistant to disease are being developed. Over the next 13 years, these advances will vastly improve the productivity of world agriculture, causing a continued glut of farm produce and an exodus of workers from the farm, particularly in the developing world.

The same technologies will have large impacts on health care, although these impacts will be delayed by the extensive testing and licensing that will be required for substances intended for human use. For example, the task of mapping the human genome is well under way. As this knowledge advances, not only will genetic birth defects become uncommon, but it will become more feasible to predict and treat many chronic and degenerative diseases such as heart disease. As the interaction of genetics and environment is better understood, advances will also be rapid against some acute diseases, with the prospect that many of today's killers will be contained by the year 2000. Although AIDS and many cancers are unlikely to be conquered within this short time frame, the knowledge gained in research on these diseases is likely to have wide-ranging impacts on the practice of medicine generally. In particular, the extraordinary progress being made by AIDS researchers in understanding the body's natural immune system will lead to medicines and treatments of unprecedented specificity and power by the year 2000.

Superconductivity: In 1986, scientists discovered a new family of materials that are superconductive (carry electric current without energy loss) at relatively high temperatures and are far more magnetic than anything previously encountered. This group of materials promises to have astonishing implications for many industries within the relatively near future.

For example, if materials can be developed that transmit electricity without loss at room temperature, there is little doubt that the whole structure of the nation's energy system will undergo radical transformation. Electricity could be generated near to coal deposits and then shipped hundreds or thousands of miles to urban areas. The efficiency of all kinds of electric motors would increase dramatically, and the size of all kinds of electric devices would shrink. Electric cars, magnetic trains, nuclear fusion, and a host of other currently unfeasible inventions could become possible.

In contrast to many less revolutionary technologies that might be expected to be integrated into the world economy relatively slowly, the potentials of superconductivity are so great that commercial applications are likely to be implemented within five to ten years. While it is too early to predict the exact consequences of such a fundamental scientific advance, superconductivity is likely by the turn of the century to be reshaping many American industries and accelerating the pace of economic change.

Technology and Change: Predictions of the impact of new technologies on the economy are highly uncertain. This is not only because technological advances themselves are hard to forecast, but also because the speed with which these technologies will be implemented will depend more on social, political, and cultural attitudes than on scientific progress. For example, improved electric motors and generators were available to industry by the 1890s, but it was not until after World War I that manufacturers began to reconfigure manufacturing plants into the more efficient layouts that were possible when each machine had its own motor. Telephones required half a century to come into wide use, yet television became universal in a single decade, as consumers rushed to purchase early models even before high-quality programming was available. The personal computer became a national market, even though the leading computer manufacturers were certain that there was little demand for them ("There is no reason for anyone to have a computer in his home," asserted Ken Olson, Chairman of the Digital Equipment Corporation, in 1977).

These vagaries of consumer acceptance of new technologies are compounded by the complexity of the changes induced by new technologies. The automobile and the truck, for example, not only revolutionized transportation, they changed the location of factories and homes, and enabled an entirely new, and more efficient, form of retailing (the regional mall) to develop. These second order effects are often the most difficult to predict, simply because the possibilities are not realized until they are exploited.

Despite these uncertainties, the technological changes on the horizon suggest that several fundamental changes are under way in the economy. First, technology is gradually overcoming the barriers of time and distance that have organized work though the centuries. In the future, technology will increasingly enable workers to choose where and when they will work. As a result, the 5-day, 40-hour, 50-week, 30-year career spent at the office or the plant will gradually become an anachronism. Work at home, work at night, work in retirement, or time off for errands, time off for child rearing and time off for vacations will be the "rules" of the future.

Second, technology is lightening the economy. As products become lighter, more intensively processed, and more durable, the per capita demand for all kinds of materials will decline. The world will not run out of oil, or metals, or food in this century or the next.

Third, technological change is so rapid that it is beyond the capacity of any single firm or nation to manage. There is no patent so valuable, no production system so advanced, and no market share so dominant that it prevents competitors from challenging an entrenched position. Because of technology, the economy of the future will be a race to stay ahead or a race to catch up. Technology will introduce change and turbulence into every industry and every job. In particular, the necessity for constant learning and constant adaptation by workers will be a certain outgrowth of technological innovation.

Renewed Productivity Growth, Particularly in Services

Productivity gains are the key to improvements in output, wages, and national income. After a boom during the early postwar period, U.S. productivity growth declined substantially during the 1970s and 1980s, with the sharpest drop beginning in 1965 (see Figure 1-14). Over the past several years, one measure of productivity improvement, increases in output per hour, has averaged a dismal 0.7 percent per year. This poor performance was largely responsible for

Figure 1-14
PRODUCTIVITY HAS DECLINED SUBSTANTIALLY
SINCE 1965
(Average For Most Recent Five Years)

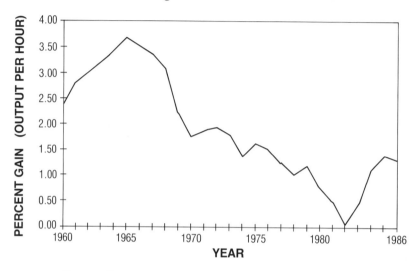

Source: Economic Report of the President, Jan. 1987

the slow growth of wages and family income that the nation has recently experienced and the stubborn persistence of poverty during the 1980s.

Various theories have been proposed to explain this weak productivity growth. Declines in the rate of capital investment, increases in the numbers of young, inexperienced workers during the 1970s, and the slowdown in the shift of workers from agriculture to industry all apparently played some part. But, despite voluminous analyses, the empirical evidence does not support any single explanation. It is clear, however, that the declines of productivity growth of the 1970s and 1980s were particularly marked in service industries (see Figure 1-15). Between 1955 and 1970, for example, output per worker in manufacturing grew at a compound rate of 2 percent per year. From 1970 to 1985, this average *accelerated* to 2.9 percent per year. In services, on the other hand, output per worker *fell* from 1.4 percent per year during the first period to −0.2 percent during the second. It was this drop in service productivity that caused the overall pattern of output per worker to slide from a 1.6 percent annual gain to only 0.5

Figure 1-15
LOW PRODUCTIVITY GROWTH IN SERVICES HAS
SLOWED U.S. ECONOMIC GROWTH

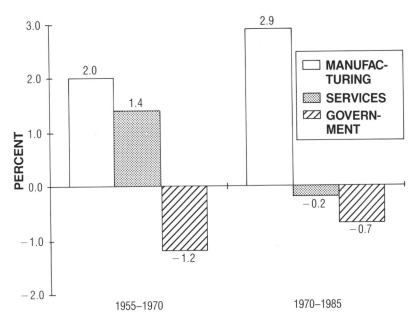

(Average Annual Percentage Increase in Output Per Worker)
Source: Wharton Econometrics, Inc.

percent. In contrast to the extensive analysis and discussion of the productivity problems in American heavy industry, the real story of the nation's productivity problems has little to do with manufacturing, which has been improving its output at an accelerating rate. Instead, it was the poor and deteriorating performance of services that dragged down output, wage gains, and national growth.

Historically, the shift from agricultural to industrial employment has accelerated the growth of productivity and output. Each worker in agriculture, for example, produces on average only about two-thirds as much as each worker in the nonfarm economy (see Figure 1-16). As workers have left agriculture for more productive jobs in factories and other industries, the economy's average productivity and output have increased.

The shift from manufacturing to services, however, does not have such beneficial effects. During the 1950s and 1960s, service workers produced about 10 percent less per worker than manufacturing workers. In 1970 each worker in the service and trade sectors of the economy produced approximately $10,900 of output, com-

Figure 1-16
OUTPUT PER WORKER IS LOWER IN FARMING THAN IN THE REST OF THE ECONOMY

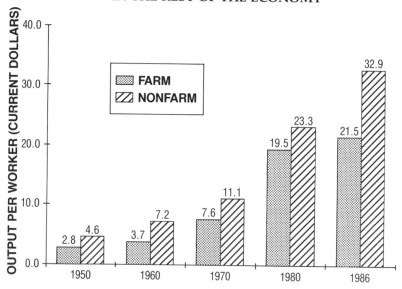

Source: Economic Report of the President, 1987

pared to $13,000 of output for each manufacturing worker. During the 1970s and 1980s, the slower growth of service industry productivity caused this ratio to decline steadily. By 1985, service industry workers were producing only $28,700 per worker, compared to $41,200 for manufacturing workers (see Figure 1-17).

The gap between output per worker in services and in manufacturing is expected to widen throughout the late 1980s and 1990s. Even if productivity growth in services rebounds sharply, it is unlikely to equal manufacturing productivity growth. As a result, the continuing shift to services in the future will impose a sustained drag on the economy.

Why have service industry productivity gains been so weak? Part of the story may be due simply to measurement problems. In some industries, such as education, health care, and many business services, there is no accepted way of measuring output and productivity. Is

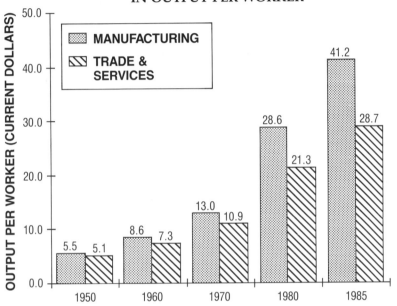

Figure 1-17
SERVICE INDUSTRIES LAG BEHIND MANUFACTURING
IN OUTPUT PER WORKER

Source: Economic Report of the President, 1987

a $50 per hour lawyer who files one short, persuasive brief more productive than a $200 per hour lawyer who files ten voluminous but irrelevant ones? Is a doctor who saves a life with an accurate emergency room diagnosis more productive than one who saves a life with years of kidney dialysis? The numbers do not capture these differences, particularly where actual outputs (e.g., student learning gains or patient health) are not comprehensively measured.

The Productivity Gains of the 1950s and 1960s

But measurement difficulties cannot completely explain the decline in service industry productivity during the last 15 years. There is no evidence, for example, that it became harder to measure service industry output during the 1970s than the 1960s. Instead, it appears that the 1950s and 1960s included periods of remarkable advances in several service industries that were not repeated during the 1970s. The slowdown of the 1970s is explained more by events that did not happen than by special circumstances peculiar to the decade.

In the retailing industry, for example, the 1950s and 1960s were marked by the proliferation of regional shopping centers and large food supermarkets. Between 1958 and 1972, the number of retail food stores declined by 26 percent, and large stores (greater than $500,000 per year) increased their share of total retail food sales from 51 to 70 percent. Although the trend toward larger stores has continued, the rate of gain has slowed simply because the process was largely complete by the early 1970s.

The transportation industry also experienced rapid productivity gains during the 1960s that were not repeated during the 1970s. In passenger transport, the jet plane increased the speed and efficiency of aircraft substantially. This helped to increase the numbers of air passengers, which led to huge gains in output and productivity. Although the 1970s saw the introduction of the jumbo jet, its impact did not equal the original change from propeller aircraft to jets. Similarly, in freight transportation, the 1960s witnessed the widespread introduction of the standardized, reusable shipping container, which enormously improved the efficiency and productivity of the trucking and ocean freight industries. Although there were further advances in the 1970s, they did not match this initial breakthrough.

The glut of new workers during the 1970s helped to retard investment that might have led to greater productivity gains in the service industries. The flood of women and young people willing to work for relatively low wages made it unnecessary for employers to develop advanced labor-saving technology. In food service, hospital care, education, and many other areas there was little pressure to develop labor-saving devices and little international competition to spur innovation.

The sluggish growth of productivity in services over the past 15 years has led many to doubt that these dispersed, low-technology industries can ever become highly automated or productive. The inherent difficulties in automating activities that occur in widely scattered locations (e.g., restaurants), and that require personal service (e.g., lawyers and doctors) seem to imply that little can be done to improve productivity in many service industries.

But the application of new and existing technologies, coupled with the declining numbers of new workers entering the workforce, suggests that industries such as health care, retailing, education, and government may be on the threshold of a new burst of productivity gains. Faced with a potential shortage of skilled workers willing to work for low wages, and responding to technological possibilities that are clearly within reach, many service industries are poised for a rebound in productivity. The next chapter discusses how some of these gains might occur.

Disinflation or Deflation in World Prices

Between 1965 and 1982, prices in the developed nations increased by more than 234 percent, an average annual increase of more than 7 percent. This long-running struggle with inflation has deeply affected the structure of the world's economy and the thinking of its economic decisionmakers. Today, assumptions about continuing inflation are built into virtually every economic choice made by consumers, governments, and industries.

During the next 13 years, however, world inflation is unlikely to reignite. Indeed, there are strong reasons to believe that the immediate future will be a mirror image of the recent past, rather than a repetition of it: price increases will continue to decelerate, and flat or even declining prices may be the rule. The most significant risks for the American and world economies in the immediate future are not from a return of inflation but from deflation.

The reasons for this projection are:

● *Excess Capacity in Oil, Food, and Natural Resources:* During the late 1970s, it became conventional wisdom that the world was running out of natural resources. Supplies of food, oil, minerals, lumber, and many other products were assumed to be growing less rapidly than population; dire projections for famines and shortages beyond the year 2000 were commonplace. The oil crises of 1973 and 1979, and the famines in Bangladesh, seemed to confirm these forecasts.

As the 1980s have progressed, the fallacy of these fears has been overwhelmingly demonstrated. Oil supplies, for example, are clearly far in excess of demand and seem likely to remain so, for at least a decade (see Figure 1-18). The great challenge for oil-producing nations is how to prevent this surplus from completely eroding OPEC's pricing structure.

Figure 1-18
OPEC CAPACITY GREATLY EXCEEDS PRODUCTION

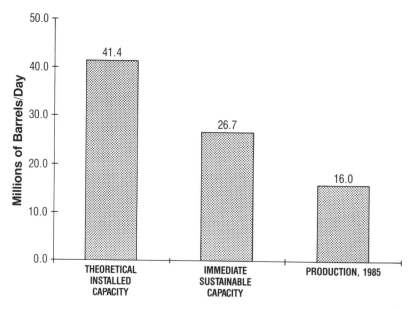

Source: Hudson Institute

Despite famines in parts of Africa and elsewhere in the world, global food supplies are also growing faster than demand. Driven by new advances in biotechnology, agricultural production in both the developed and developing world has been growing rapidly. Between 1971 and 1984, world food production rose at a compound rate of 2.4 percent annually, compared to world population growth of only 1.9 percent per year.

This relatively rapid growth of food production increased world nutritional standards in many countries. It also drove down world agricultural prices, continuing a trend that has been under way for the last 35 years (see Figure 1-19).

In the 1980s, a growing number of Asian nations that were once large importers of grain achieved self-sufficiency or net export status. India had a large surplus of wheat in 1985, and Indonesia was

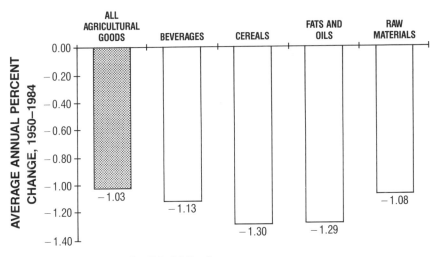

Figure 1-19
THE PRICES OF AGRICULTURAL GOODS HAVE BEEN DECLINING

Source: The World Bank

self-sufficient in rice. China shifted from being a major importer of food grains in the 1970s to being an exporter in the 1980s. Even Bangladesh was able substantially to reduce its cereal imports in the 1980s. Both government policy changes and improved systems of cultivation and agricultural management were responsible for these shifts.

Over the next decade, this trend toward self-sufficiency in the developing world may accelerate. There is growing recognition that previous policies that penalized or constrained agriculture have failed, and a new willingness to liberalize these restrictions is emerging in many developing nations. At the same time, investments in agriculture and the application of new technologies promise to improve yields substantially, with the greatest relative gains coming in the developing countries.

These developments suggest that over the next several years world supplies of food grains may be in substantial oversupply, as more nations achieve their goal of self-sufficiency, while the industrial countries continue to protect and subsidize their agriculture. This oversupply will continue to hold down food price increases.

In addition to food and oil, many other raw materials are currently in oversupply. For example, supplies of tin, copper, iron ore, and other metals have far exceeded demands in recent years. Continuing investments in mineral production by governments in developing countries seeking to increase exports promise to prolong this oversupply condition indefinitely, keeping downward pressure on commodity prices.

• *Excess Capacity in Manufactured Goods:* The glut in raw materials is echoed in manufactured products. In the steel industry, for example, world production capacity stood at some 570 million tons in 1985, compared to consumption of only 450 million tons. For automobiles, the picture is similar, with world capacity of about 42–44 million vehicles, compared to demand of about 35 million. In semiconductors, capacity utilization stands at about 70 percent, compared to almost 100 percent in 1984. Though the current recovery has been under way for more than five years, excess capacity is still present in many other industries as well, including textiles, heavy equipment, and computers.

Of course, market forces will eventually correct these imbalances, as the least efficient and unprofitable firms are forced to reduce production. But intervention by governments seems likely to prolong the overcapacity. Among developing nations, the desire to industrialize by building world-scale heavy production facilities is leading to continued investments in steel, textiles, and other goods. In automobiles, national pride and beliefs in the importance of the industry as an engine of growth have slowed the industry's consolidation, at the same time that many developing countries are insisting on more local production as the price of access to their markets. More recently, the semiconductor industry has been the subject of similar intervention by governments, as the U.S. and Japan have each taken action to preserve and build their industries, despite worldwide overcapacity.

These government-preserved excesses will continue to depress the prices of manufactured goods as long as they persist, with autos, steel, textiles, and semiconductors feeling the greatest impacts.

• *Worldwide Labor Surpluses:* Although the U.S. labor force will be growing slowly through the balance of the century, the world picture is much different. Three decades ago, advances in health care led to dramatic drops in infant mortality and an acceleration in world population growth. These millions of children have grown up, moved to the city, gone to school, and are now looking for jobs. In 1984, for example, almost half of the residents of middle income developing countries lived in cities, and half of all teenagers were enrolled in school. As recently as 1965, only a third of the residents of these countries were urbanized and a only a fifth of teenagers attended high school.

This widespread pattern of urbanization and more universal education is increasing the size of the world labor market at an extraordinary rate. Between 1985 and 2000, the world labor force will grow at a compound rate of more than 2 percent, adding more than 600 million new job seekers to the world workforce.

Not all of these workers will be unskilled laborers and mill hands. In the developing world, the share of the population attending college has more than doubled during the last 20 years and continues to increase. The trend toward increased trade, travel, and immigration will mean that these better-educated workers will be in competition for the world's supply of highly-skilled jobs and that wage competition across international borders in all kinds of occupations will become more intense. This wage competition will help to hold down wage increases, dampening inflationary pressures.

• *The Failure of Governments to Stimulate Demand Along With Production:* Surpluses of production capacity and labor would not necessarily lead to stable or falling prices, if they were matched by parallel increases in demand. But government decisionmakers, emerging from more than a decade of potentially catastrophic inflation, have been reluctant to stimulate their economies aggressively to absorb excess capacity. This has been especially true of Japan and West Germany, where both fiscal and monetary policies have been cautious throughout the 1980s. The United States has run much more stimulative fiscal and monetary policies, but is currently retreating from both.

For different reasons, the economies of a substantial portion of the developing world have also been slow to grow. In Latin America, the debt crisis has slowed international lending and produced a crisis of confidence that has undermined economic activity. In parts of Asia, political instability has created a similar pause in growth. For nations that are dependent on natural resources, the glut of commodities has eroded the basis for industrialization and economic advance, making growth more difficult to achieve.

Instead of macroeconomic stimulus, governments have generally sought to capture market share in industrial products, all hoping to generate export-led growth. These policies, which seem sensible on a country-by-country basis, cannot collectively succeed. By adding to production capability without stimulating demand, they are likely to lead to relatively slow worldwide growth. Slow growth, coupled with huge excesses in capacity to produce raw materials and industrial goods, is likely to hold down worldwide price increases throughout the next 13 years and could degenerate into a deflationary spiral.

Increased Competition In Product, Service, and Labor Markets

For a number of reasons, the world economy has become more competitive in recent years, and this trend promises to continue until the year 2000 and beyond. The integration of global markets, excess production capacity, the rapidly growing world labor force, the decline of labor unions, and the general deregulation of industry by many western governments are all contributing to the competitive trend. For both firms and nations, increased competition means that there will be relentless pressure to change and adapt to new markets and technologies. It also means that it will be increasingly difficult to create jobs and profits based on traditional market shares, technological advantages, or proprietary knowledge.

For the United States, it means that maintaining world leadership in any industry or technology will be a ceaseless struggle that will require extraordinary individual and collective national effort. In earlier eras, changes in the economic power of the British or Roman empires required centuries to play themselves out. The new competitiveness of the world economy means that, in economic terms, great changes in America's postwar economic power could come in a matter of decades or even years, depending on how well the nation continues to innovate, adapt, and grow.

There are five factors that are most responsible for the increasing competitiveness of the world economy:

● *Integrated World Markets:* Competition that used to be limited by geography now knows no national boundaries. Protected national monopolies that once could dictate the prices of cars or the wages of auto workers have given way to competitive prices and wage rates. Similarly, the opening of world financial markets means that the cost of capital is becoming more equal in various countries.

● *Oversupply of Production Capacity:* The glut of natural resources, manufactured goods, and educated workers means that the competition among producers and workers will be relentless.

● *The Decline of Labor Union Wage-Setting Power:* In the United States in particular, labor unions control a shrinking fraction of the industrial workforce. While this trend may not continue indefinitely, its impacts on competition in labor markets will continue to be felt throughout the next 13 years. Whether a pattern of contract "givebacks" persists or not, the wage premium exacted by labor union members in manufacturing industries will shrink as nonunion companies, both in and outside the United States, compete for jobs once controlled by unionized employers.

● *Deregulation of Industry:* Over the past decade, governments in many industrialized countries have reduced their intervention into their domestic economies. In the United States, for example, the transportation industries have been largely freed from regulation; supervision of telecommunications, financial services, and energy has been relaxed or abandoned, and antitrust enforcement of restrictions on mergers and acquisitions has become less restrictive. In the future, it seems possible that in the United States other utilities such as electricity may also be freed from some types of regulation; other nations may follow the U.S. lead in deregulating airlines, trucking, and telecommunications.

In combination, these steps to eliminate governments from markets have made the world's economy increasingly competitive, and the effects of this renewed competition are still working their way through the global system.

● *Privatization:* Along with the relaxation of government regulation has come a parallel effort to divest government from the direct provision of goods and services. In European countries where nationally-owned firms are commonplace, a significant effort is under way to return many of these firms to the private sector. In the United States, where there is little nationalized industry, the action is at the state level, where an increasing variety of government services are being contracted to private companies.

In combination, these efforts to rely on private companies and unregulated markets have intensified and stimulated new competition and new innovation in many once-lethargic industries. Although the political enthusiasm for further deregulation may have peaked, the impacts of what has already occurred will echo through the U.S. and world economies for the balance of the century.

CHAPTER 2
Scenarios For The Year 2000

Three Projections of the Future

In order to evaluate policy options, this section outlines three scenarios for the development of the U.S. economy between 1987 and 2000.[1] Although these scenarios might be characterized as high, middle, and low growth, they are not intended simply to bracket a range of possible growth rates. Rather they are meant to illustrate the forces that will be shaping American industries and the impact that different policy choices could have on the U.S. economy in the future.

Many factors are constant in all three scenarios. For example, each is characterized by moderate inflation, improvement in the trade and budget deficits, and increased integration of the world economy. There is no disaster scenario in which world war, a hole in the ozone, or an unchecked AIDS epidemic creates catastrophic change.

The scenarios are distinguished from each other primarily on the basis of policy differences: how much does protectionism and poor allocation of investment slow down world growth?; how rapidly are entrenched institutions and habit-bound individuals willing to adapt to new technologies?; how intensively does the nation invest in its primary asset—human capital?

Although different factors are emphasized in each scenario, the actual path that the economy follows is likely to be a blend of elements from each. For policymakers, the value of the scenarios is not so much to define the most likely future, but to illustrate the opportunities and risks they face under various conditions, to provide

---

[1]The descriptions of the U.S. economic future presented here were developed using the Wharton Econometrics, Inc. long-term model of the U.S. economy. This is the same model used by the U.S. Department of Labor for its forecasts of the U.S. job market. Of course, the assumptions incorporated into the model are solely the responsibility of the Hudson Institute.

a numerical basis for testing alternative choices, and to identify the issues that most urgently deserve attention.

The baseline or "surprise-free" scenario represents a modest improvement in the rate of growth that the nation experienced between 1970 and 1985. Despite markedly better trends in inflation and productivity, the U.S. economy does not return to the boom times of the 1950s and 1960s. Slow labor force growth is only partly offset by productivity gains, and imperfect coordination among the world's governments leads to only moderate rates of world growth. Turbulence in world economic affairs—with rapid fluctuations in the value of the dollar, the growth policies of other nations, and the prices of oil and other commodities—causes periodic recessions that hold total growth to just under three percent per year.

In contrast, the "world deflation" scenario focuses on the possibility that a worldwide glut of production capacity in food, minerals, manufactured products, and labor could lead to a sustained price deflation and sluggish economic growth. World governments, chastened by a decade and a half of inflation, are slow to recognize the new economic realities and unwilling to undertake coordinated efforts to respond to them. The U.S., whose huge trade deficit has been the world's growth engine during the early 1980s, moves toward balance in its trade and fiscal accounts, but, in doing so, slips into a severe recession. Without U.S. stimulus, the rest of the world slides into a series of recessions that lead to increased protectionism and beggar-thy-neighbor trade, monetary, and fiscal policies. Despite repeated efforts to coordinate stimulative actions, the world is unable to reflate on a sustained basis. Growth averages only 1.6 percent per year over the period.

The third scenario, "technology boom," suggests that U.S. economic growth may rebound to levels that compare with the first two decades following World War II. Coordinated international monetary, fiscal, and trade policies succeed in smoothing world business cycles. Renewed public and private lending to developing nations and low oil prices trigger rapid growth in much of the Third World. In the U.S., high rates of investment in both physical and human capital, coupled with low inflation, low resource prices, lower taxes, and less government intervention combine to produce a boom in productivity that raises real after-tax per capita income by almost 50 percent over the 15-year period. The widespread application of computer and communications technologies, along with sweeping changes in the organization and delivery of health, financial, education, and other services, and marked improvement in the trade and budget deficits. leads to an astonishing rebirth of the U.S. economy, with growth averaging 4 percent per year over the period. Table 2-1 summarizes the major assumptions and outcomes of the three scenarios in numerical detail and compares them with previous periods. The table underscores several key points about the U.S. economy over the next 13 years:

● *U.S. Growth and World Growth Are Tightly Linked:* The strong historical correlation between world growth and U.S. growth continues through the balance of the century. In the baseline forecast, the U.S. grows at about 2.9 percent, compared to 3.1 percent for the world. Both the high and low forecasts show a similar tight linkage between the United States and world economies.

● *U.S. Manufacturing Employment Declines While Services Grow:* Despite strong export growth and substantial production increases, manufacturing jobs decline in all scenarios. Whether the U.S. and world economies are booming in an open trading environment or growing slowly in an atmosphere of protectionism and nationalistic trading patterns, U.S. manufacturing jobs decrease. Although fewer goods-producing jobs are lost if the U.S. pursues a protectionist trade policy, the gains do not offset the huge losses in the service economy in the slow growth, protectionist scenario.

The decline of manufacturing employment that occurs in all scenarios represents a departure from past trends. Until 1979, manufacturing jobs were a declining share of U.S. employment, but the absolute numbers were steady or rising. For the balance of the century, manufacturing jobs are declining both absolutely and relatively.

● *The Key to Domestic Economic Growth is a Rebound in Productivity, Particularly in Services:* The similarity in economic growth rates between 1955–1970, 1970–1985, and 1985–2000 masks dramatic changes in the nature of the economy. To offset the decline in the rate of labor force growth, the nation must substantially increase its productivity. In the baseline scenario, output per worker, which was an anemic 0.7 percent from 1970 to 1985, more than doubles to 1.5 percent per year,

Table 2-1
THE U.S. ECONOMY IN THE YEAR 2000

	1955		1970		1985		2000 Base		2000 Low		2000 High	
	Level	Change*%	Level	Change*%	Level	Change*%	Level	Change*%	Level	Change*%	Level	Change*%
Non-Communist World GDP (bill. 82 $)	NA	NA	4842	NA	7745	3.18%	12204	3.1%	9546	1.4%	13057	3.5%
U.S. GNP (bill. 82 $)	1495	NA	2416	3.25%	3570	2.64%	5463	2.9%	4537	1.6%	6431	4.0%
U.S. GNP (bill. current $)	406	NA	1016	6.30%	3988	9.55%	9963	6.3%	5344	2.0%	12631	8.0%
Unemployment Rate (%)	4.4	—	4.9	—	7.1	—	7.0	—	9.9	—	5.9	—
GNP Deflator (1982=100)	27.2	NA	42.0	2.94%	111.7	6.74%	182.4	3.3%	117.8	0.4%	196.4	3.8%
Employment (millions)	62.2	NA	78.6	1.58%	107.2	2.09%	131.0	1.3%	122.4	0.9%	139.9	1.8%
Manufacturing	16.9	NA	19.4	0.92%	19.3	-0.02%	17.2	-0.8%	18.0	-0.4%	18.1	-0.4%
Commercial & Other Services	27.0	NA	38.2	2.34%	62.0	3.29%	84.3	2.1%	76.5	1.4%	88.7	2.4%
Productivity												
(output/worker, 82 $)	24.1	NA	30.2	1.52%	33.3	0.66%	41.7	1.5%	37.1	0.7%	46.0	2.2%
Manufacturing	19.4	NA	26.2	2.01%	40.4	2.93%	71.4	3.9%	58.0	2.5%	81.3	4.8%
Commercial & Other Services	24.9	NA	30.6	1.41%	29.9	-0.17%	34.1	0.9%	30.4	0.1%	38.2	1.6%
Fed. Surplus (bill. curr. $)	4.4	—	-12.4	—	-200.8	—	-110.0	—	-170.1	—	-40.7	—
Deficit/GNP (absolute number)	0.29%	—	0.51%	—	5.62%	—	2.01%	—	3.75%	—	0.63%	—
Current Account Balance (bill. curr. $)	0.4	—	2.3	—	-116.8	—	14.8	—	12.5	—	32.6	—
Exports (bill. 82 $)	76.9	NA	178.3	5.77%	359.8	4.79%	800.2	5.5%	500.6	2.2%	958.8	6.8%
Imports (bill. 82 $)	76.9	NA	208.3	6.87%	467.8	5.54%	773.9	3.4%	482.4	0.2%	952.5	4.9%
Interest Rates (moodys corp bond rate)**	3.1	NA	4.9	NA	10.0	NA	7.2	NA	5.1	NA	7.3	NA
Average Compensation Per Worker (Thou 82$)	13.4	NA	18.7	2.27%	19.8	0.39%	25.6	1.7%	22.0	0.7%	27.6	2.2%
Consumption Per Capita (Thou. 82 $)	5.3	NA	7.3	2.13%	9.6	1.89%	12.5	1.8%	10.7	0.7%	14.3	2.7%
Disposable Income Per Capita (Thou. 82 $)	5.7	NA	8.1	2.38%	10.5	1.69%	13.5	1.7%	11.5	0.6%	15.6	2.7%

*Average Annual Gain **Average For Period
Source: Hudson Institute.

Figure 2-1
U.S. PRODUCTIVITY REBOUNDS OFFSETTING
SLOWER LABOR FORCE GROWTH

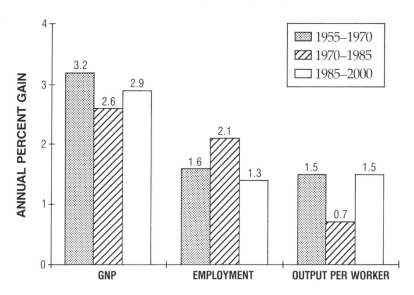

Source: Wharton Econometrics, Hudson Institute

equal to the rate that prevailed from 1955–1970 (see Figure 2-1). This rebound stems from a modest improvement in manufacturing productivity, from 3.4 percent per year in the most recent 15-year period to 3.9 percent from 1985–2000. This is coupled with a sharp turnaround in service industry productivity, which climbs from -0.2 percent to +0.9 percent. By contrast, in the deflation scenario, productivity continues to stumble along at the rates of the 1970–1985 period, causing the economy to grow by less than 2 percent per year. This projected gain in productivity is the key, not only to the performance of the economy over the next 13 years, but to the increases that are forecast in compensation, personal income, and the quality of the jobs of the year 2000. Throughout the 1970s and early 1980s, the United States managed to sustain a rising standard of living, by increasing the number of people at work and by borrowing from abroad and from the future. These props under the nation's consumption will eventually reach their limits: there will be relatively fewer young people and homemakers who will enter the workforce during the 1990s, and the burden of consumer, government, and international debt cannot be expanded indefinitely. Instead, the nation must find ways to increase its output per worker, particularly in the service industries that will increasingly dominate the economy.

● *U.S. Trade Accounts Move Toward Balance:* Although the different scenarios show widely dispersed rates of growth of imports and exports, the U.S. current account balance improves under all conditions. This is due both to the revaluation of the dollar that has already taken place against other currencies and to improving productivity in manufacturing industries. Under the baseline scenario, the U.S. current account balance is in the black by some $14 billion by the year 2000, although the nation has incurred a cumulative debt to the rest of the world of some $900 billion during the period. Though this cumulative debt seems staggering, it is only 11 percent of U.S. GNP at its peak. The favorable trend in the current account balance, coupled with the large size of the U.S. economy and the difficulty that foreign holders of U.S. dollars have in investing such large sums elsewhere in the world, enables the U.S. to finance its debt burden with less difficulty than has been feared.

● *The U.S. Budget Deficit Declines:* Along with the improvement in the trade deficit comes a decline in the budget deficit. Even without any major tax increases, growth in GNP and a large surplus in the Social Security Trust Fund cut the federal budget deficit to $18 billion by 1995.

● *Inflation Remains Under Control:* Under the baseline scenario, inflation increases by an average of 3.2 percent per year over the 1985–2000 period. This compares to only 0.3 percent in the deflation scenario and 3.9 percent in the boom scenario. The excess world capacity in labor, goods, and services prevents inflation from resuming the pace of the 1970s.

● *Unemployment Remains Stubbornly High:* The baseline scenario forecasts unemployment at just over 7 percent in the year 2000, despite the relatively slow growth of the labor force projected over the period. In the deflation scenario, unemployment climbs above 9 percent, while, even in the boom scenario, unemployment is reduced only to 5.9 percent. High growth draws more women and immigrants into the U.S. labor force at the same time that substantial numbers of the least-skilled remain unable to find jobs in the new high-productivity, high-technology economy.

● *Disposable Income Increases Moderately:* Disposable personal income per person, the best single measure of how rapidly society is

Table 2-2
GOODS PRODUCTION WILL SHRINK FURTHER BY THE YEAR 2000
(Output in Millions of Current Dollars)

	1985		2000		CHANGE (1985–2000)	
	Amount	Share	Amount	Share	Amount	Percent
TOTAL	$3,897	100.00%	$9,965	100.00%	$6,068	155.69%
---------Goods ---------						
Total	1222.1	31.36%	2469.5	25.05%	1274.3	104.27%
Farm, Forest, Fishing	98.2	2.52%	301.8	3.03%	203.6	207.37%
Mining	118.0	3.03%	129.1	1.30%	11.1	9.37%
Construction	192.2	4.93%	416.3	4.18%	224.1	116.57%
Manufacturing	813.7	20.88%	1649.3	16.55%	835.6	102.69%
Durable	479.1	12.29%	993.9	9.97%	514.8	107.46%
Nondurable	334.6	8.59%	655.4	6.58%	320.8	95.86%
---------Services---------						
Total	2053.1	52.68%	5665.3	56.85%	3612.2	175.94%
Fin. Ins. & Real Estate	624.9	16.03%	1688.9	16.95%	1064.0	170.26%
Wholesale & Retail Trade ..	667.5	17.13%	1881.5	18.88%	1214.0	181.88%
Other Services............	626.1	16.06%	1818.1	18.24%	1192.0	190.41%
Transport. Utils. Comm ...	134.7	3.46%	267.8	2.78%	142.1	105.52%
--Government & Other* --						
Total	622.1	15.96	1803.5	18.10%	1181.3	189.88%

*Excludes government services such as transportation and health care included in other categories.
Source: Hudson Institute.

improving its standard of living, grows by 1.7 percent per year under the baseline scenario, almost precisely the rate at which it grew between 1970 and 1985. The boom scenario boosts this index to 2.7 percent, 13 percent above its level during the 1955–1970 period. Low growth during the deflation scenario causes disposable income to creep up by only 0.6 percent per year, which would be worse than at any time in the postwar era.

The Surprise-Free Scenario: Outcomes and Impacts

The similarities among the scenarios illustrate some of the fundamental forces shaping the U.S. economy. A more detailed look at the surprise-free scenario sheds more light on the most important changes ahead. Two areas deserve the greatest attention: the changing structure of the economy and the prospects for greater productivity growth.

The Changing Structure of the U.S. Economy

Between 1985 and 2000, employment and output in goods production will continue to decline (see Tables 2-2 and 2-3). By the

Table 2-3
EMPLOYMENT IN GOODS PRODUCTION WILL DECLINE BY THE YEAR 2000
(Millions of Workers)

	1985		2000		CHANGE (1985–2000)	
	Number*	Share	Number	Share	Number	Percent
TOTAL	107.16	100.00%	130.96	100.00%	23.81	22.22%
- - - - - - - - -Goods - - - - - - - - -						
Total	28.21	26.32%	25.74	19.65%	−2.47	−8.76%
Farm, Forest, Fishing	3.14	2.93%	2.67	2.04%	−0.47	−14.88%
Mining	0.97	0.90%	0.79	0.60%	−0.18	−18.68%
Construction	4.66	4.35%	5.06	3.86%	0.40	8.52%
Manufacturing	19.44	18.14%	17.22	13.15%	−2.22	−11.42%
Durable	11.58	10.81%	10.51	8.02%	−1.08	−9.28%
Nondurable	7.86	7.34%	6.72	5.13%	−1.15	−14.57%
- - - - - - - - -Services- - - - - - - - -						
Total	72.62	67.77%	96.51	73.69%	23.89	32.90%
Fin. Ins. & Real Estate	5.92	5.53%	8.12	6.20%	2.19	37.02%
Wholesale & Retail Trade ..	23.19	21.64%	30.37	23.19%	7.18	30.95%
Regulated Industries	5.29	4.94%	5.76	4.40%	0.47	8.92%
Other Services............	21.92	20.46%	32.16	24.56%	10.24	46.71%
Government	16.30	15.21%	20.10	15.35%	3.81	23.37%

*Excludes Self-employment
Source: Hudson Institute.

year 2000, manufacturing will employ 2.2 million fewer workers than it does today, and only 14 percent of all U.S. employees will work in manufacturing industries. Both durables and nondurables will shed more than one million workers, with the biggest losses coming in primary metals (−346,000), textiles (−243,000), and motor vehicles (−143,000).

Manufacturing output will increase, but at a much slower rate than GNP, so that by the year 2000 manufacturing output (measured in year 2000 dollars) will shrink to only 17 percent of GNP, compared to 21 percent today. Services, including government services, will account for three-fourths of the nominal economy, up from 69 percent today.

The relative positions of manufacturing and finance illustrate the changes ahead. As recently as 1965, the finance, insurance, and real estate industries contributed only half as much value to the economy as did manufacturing, 14 percent compared to 28 percent. By the year 2000, these financial services will account for $1.7 trillion of GNP, surpassing the $1.6 trillion total of manufacturing. Similar declines will take place in the shares of employment and GNP accounted for by most types of goods production, including mining and construction. Farming continues to decline in employment share, but a rebound in farm prices from the depressed levels of 1985 raises agriculture's share of the economy's output.

On the services side of the ledger, virtually every subcategory will show large gains in employment and share of output, with the fastest gainers including wholesale and retail trade, and the other services category that includes health care and business services. One telling measure of the change ahead is that the trade and service sectors will *add* more jobs between 1985 and the year 2000 than now exist in all U.S. manufacturing.

In the retail category, restaurants and bars hire 2.4 million new workers, while food stores gain 1.1 million, and general merchandise adds 800,000. In the services category, the biggest gainers are business services (3.6 million) and health services (3.1 million). In finance, insurance, and real estate, the most new jobs are in banking (591,000) and insurance (559,000).

The Impacts of the Shift To Services

What do these shifts mean for the nation? Although the decline of goods production and the shift to services are not the ominous trends portrayed in the press, they will have a number of far-reaching impacts. The distribution of earnings, the structure of world trade, union activity, the cyclicality of the economy, and many other factors will be affected. Some of the most obvious impacts of the trends will be:

• *The Typical Workplace Will Be Smaller and Most New Jobs Will Be in Small Businesses:* Because services are typically located near consumers, each worksite in service industries tends to be smaller than in manufacturing. For example, the average manufacturing establishment employs some 60 people, compared to only 11 for the typical service establishment (see Figure 2-2).

Because all employment growth will be in service industries, most new jobs will be created by small businesses. Between 1978 and 1982, for example, more than half of all new jobs were created by firms with fewer than 100 employees. The smallest firms (those with less than 20 workers) represented only one-fifth of all employment, but created two-fifths of all net new jobs (see Table 2-4).

This concentration of new jobs in small businesses and small establishments will have major implications for the sociology and structure of work. For example, management systems designed for large bureaucratic organizations may increasingly give way to systems with delegated responsibility that employ small team concepts

Figure 2-2
SERVICE INDUSTRY ESTABLISHMENTS ARE SMALLER

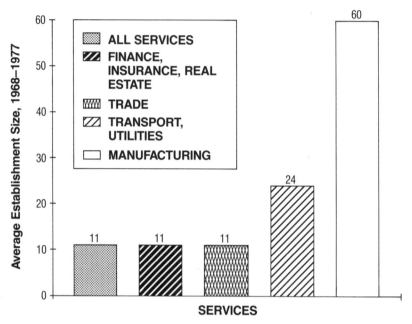

Source: Mark Granovetter, American Sociological Review, Vol. 49, 1984

to motivate and manage people. Unionization may be more difficult, both because of the dispersion of workplaces and the closeness of

Table 2-4
MOST NEW JOBS HAVE BEEN CREATED BY SMALL FIRMS
(numbers in millions)

	Jobs in 1976		New Jobs Created 1976–1982	
	Number	Share	Number	Share
Total	76.0	100%	11.9	100%
Firm Size				
0–19 Employees	15.6	21%	4.6	39%
20–99	12.8	17%	1.7	14%
100–499	10.8	14%	1.2	10%
500+	36.7	48%	4.5	38%

Source: Office of Advocacy, U.S. Small Business Administration, unpublished data.

management and employees. Training may be more expensive at small work sites and less likely to be provided by small employers operating with lower overhead.

● *Wages May Become Less Equally Distributed*

While the stereotypes of a disappearing middle class in the service economy are exaggerated, the shift to services will have some impact on the distribution of wages in the economy. As noted earlier, wages in the slower-growing or shrinking manufacturing and government sectors are more equally distributed than those in the expanding service sector. While the impact of the shift has not yet been significant, it could become so.

If service industry productivity rises rapidly, wages are also likely to rise quickly, and the shift to service jobs with less equally distributed earnings may not create much concern. But in combination with relatively slow growth of productivity in services, the shift to these industries with less equal wage distribution is likely to ignite significant political and social controversy. Unless service industry productivity surges ahead very quickly, these industries are likely to be the next battleground for unionization or perhaps for government intervention, to help equalize incomes through tax policy or minimum wages.

● *Part-time Work Will Increase*

While the 40-hour workweek has remained standard in manufacturing, this is not the case in many service industries. In retail trade, for example, the average workweek fell to only 29 hours in 1986. In the finance industry, the average is 36 hours, while those in the miscellaneous services category put in only 32 hours per week. As a result of the shorter hours in these large and growing industries, the average workweek for all those in the economy has dropped from 40 hours in 1948 to less than 35 hours today.

Because services must usually be performed when and where the customer wants them, the trend toward flexible schedules, part-time workers, and shorter hours is likely to continue. Gradually, the less-than-forty hour week will become the rule. While it seems unlikely that the short workweek will be officially sanctioned or legislated, the nation will slowly establish it as the de facto standard. By the year 2000, this evolution may lead to reductions in the workweek of "full-time" workers and revisions in benefit structures. Currently, for example, part-time workers often receive lower levels

Figure 2-3
SERVICES MODERATE THE BUSINESS CYCLE

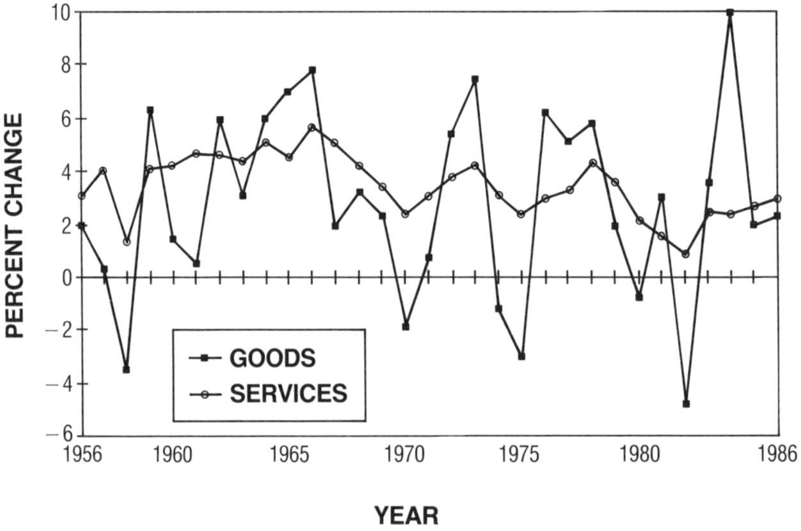

Source: Economic Report of the President, 1987

of fringe benefits such as vacation, health, and retirement. If the 35-
or 30-hour week becomes universal, this two-tier benefit structure
will no longer seem justifiable and may begin to erode. Unionization
in the service industries might hasten such a development.

• *Reduced Cyclicality in the Economy*

No foreseeable change in the nation's industrial structure will
eliminate the business cycle. But the trend toward service employment will certainly moderate it. Between 1956 and 1986, services have
never had a recession, and their annual growth rate has swung only
between .9 and 5.7 percent. The goods economy, on the other hand,
has been in recession in six of the 30 years, with growth swinging
wildly from -4.8 to 10 percent (see Figure 2-3).

As the economy becomes more and more dominated by services,
the severity of recessions should be reduced; in the same way, the
explosive growth that has sometimes been triggered by a boom in
goods production should also be moderated. As services grow above
three-fourths of the economy, their balance wheel effect should
moderate swings in demand.

● *The Nature of World Trade Will Be Altered*

Imports and exports of goods still dominate world trade, although services have become more important in recent years. Despite growth in service exports and recent efforts to reduce international barriers to service imports, it is unlikely that trade in services will overtake goods-trading for the foreseeable future. The reality is that very few services can be transported across international boundaries. With the exception of transportation and tourism, the great majority of international trade in services is not really trade at all, but simply money moving across international borders as interest, dividends, remittances, and capital investments.

Because the value of services tends to be created mostly in home countries near to customers, the importance of goods-trading among the most advanced industrial countries may decline in the years after 2000, as their economies become dominated by service industries. A greater fraction of world trade will then consist of goods exchanges among developing countries, while the post-industrial countries trade people, knowledge, and capital.

As this trend develops, it may make it more complicated for developing nations to use traditional goods exports as their avenue for development. As the advanced countries come to place relatively low values on imported goods and high value on services that they produce themselves, many developing countries may find that it is much more difficult to build substantial export industries by selling goods to each other. While the peaking of goods-trading among developed countries should not begin until after the turn of the century, potential difficulties for developing countries relying on exports may begin before then.

● *Rapid Growth Will Be Harder to Achieve*

Although productivity is expected to improve substantially in service industries toward the end of the next decade, these gains will not prevent the services from being a drag on the U.S. economy through much of the next 13 years. The relatively lower output of workers in service industries today, coupled with the moderate projected rates of productivity growth in the years immediately ahead, means that, in the near-term, economic growth may be sluggish. Only a remarkable, and unlikely, near-term rebound in service industry productivity could improve this outlook.

Improved Productivity Gains, Especially in Services

Slow growth of the labor force, increased capital investment, and better education and training, coupled with deregulation, privatization, and less government intervention into the economy may lead to a rebound in the productivity of the economy over the next 13 years. Part of the gains will come in the traditional manufacturing industries that have been spurred by foreign competition to adapt new technologies (e.g., robots) and systems of organization (e.g., just-in-time inventory) to improve their quality, cut costs, and raise output.

But by themselves, these gains in manufacturing productivity will not be enough to offer most Americans a higher standard of living, simply because manufacturing is such a small and shrinking share of U.S. production. The service industries, which will be 75 percent of the economy by the year 2000, must increase their productivity performance dramatically if the nation is to prosper. The task of improving American international competitiveness in manufactured goods is of secondary importance, compared with challenge of raising service industry productivity.

This point is illustrated by analysis of the structure of future GNP growth, compared with past growth. Between 1955 and 1970, for example, manufacturing contributed about one-fifth to GNP, of which two-thirds came from productivity gain and one-third from employment growth. Between 1970 and 1985, manufacturing's contribution climbed to one-fourth, all of which came from productivity gains. Over the next 15 years, manufacturing will again contribute about one-fourth of the economy's growth, which will consist of a 30 percent gain in productivity offset by a 7 percent decline in employment (see Figure 2-4).

On the service side of the ledger, the picture is similar. In the 1955–1970 period, services (including government services) accounted for 80 percent of GNP growth, of which employment accounted for three-fifths. In the 1970s, the nonmanufacturing sector contributed 80 percent of GNP gains, with all of the gains coming from employment, while productivity actually fell slightly. In the next 15 years, nonmanufacturing industries will contribute about three-fourths of the economy's growth, of which three-fifths will be due to employment gains and two-fifths to productivity increases. Without these substantial gains in service industry productivity, the economy would grow by less than 2 percent per year.

Figure 2-4
PRODUCTIVITY GAINS IN SERVICES ARE THE KEY TO FUTURE ECONOMIC GROWTH

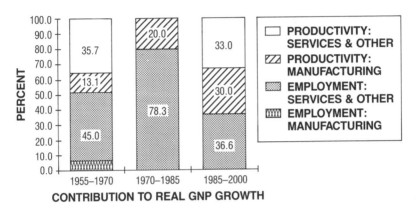

CONTRIBUTION TO REAL GNP GROWTH

Source: Hudson Institute

How might such a major improvement in service industry productivity occur? Past examples provide some clues. When the supermarket chains replaced the small mom-and-pop grocers with large, high-volume, bar-code check-out stores, they employed technology, size, and standardization to reach a new level of productivity. When McDonald's and other franchisers created their standardized, limited-menu, fast food outlets with production-line kitchens and push button cash registers, they enormously increased the productivity of an industry that had been characterized by slow, cook-to-order kitchens and inefficient dining room service. In each case, standardized, more capital-intensive systems were created that relied on customers to perform some of the functions previously performed by the service provider.

Many other service industries are ripe for such changes. Consider these possibilities:

HEALTH CARE: Throughout the postwar era, health care has been driven primarily by the desires of doctors and hospitals to improve the quality of medical care and treatment. Cost control and productivity gains have been of secondary importance. Until very recently, the emphasis has been on saving lives, rather than on saving money.

Attempts by the government, employers, and large health care providers to control costs are likely to shift attention toward technologies and systems that improve efficiency and reduce expenses, without sacrificing the quality of care. When the large institutions that are increasingly in control of the health-care industry begin to respond to these new incentives, radical improvements in productivity may be possible. For example:

• *The Self-diagnostic Health Clinic:* In the 1990s, patients of a modern HMO might receive sophisticated diagnosis and even some forms of treatment with limited intervention by doctors, nurses, or clerical support personnel. A patient might enter a clinic and identify himself with an electronic card containing his complete computerized medical history and automatic billing information. After responding to a series of questions posed by a computer, he would submit to a series of self-adminstered, non-invasive tests (e.g., temperature, blood pressure, blood chemistry, urinanalysis, and perhaps others based on cheap magnetic scanning devices). Finally, he might receive a preliminary diagnosis and be issued an unsigned prescription for medication. Only when this automated process was complete, would he see a nurse or a doctor. Routine treatments might be cheaper, less time-consuming, more private, and more effective than those offered in today's clinics and doctors' offices.

• *The Automated Nursing Home:* Cooking, cleaning, personal care, and other low-productivity tasks are the most costly aspects of nursing care. But the same technologies that promise to automate factories by the year 2000—robotics, machine vision, artificial intelligence—have application in this rapidly-growing, labor-intensive service industry. Advanced robots capable of assisting patients with walking and feeding, cleaning floors, reading books or newspapers, or other tasks are only a few years away. These assistants will not be thought of as threatening or impersonal robots, but as personal tools capable of enhancing the diminished capabilities of nursing home residents.

RETAILING: The advances in efficiency brought by regional malls, supermarkets, and fast food restaurants have begun to reach their natural limits, as congestion, sales transaction times, and inventory carrying charges place limits on further productivity gains based on store size or customer traffic volumes. But new forms and systems for retailing are on the horizon. For example:

• *The Direct Sales Manufacturer:* Historically, manufacturers have sold to wholesalers, who have resold goods to retailers, who have sold to final buyers. Goods are typically handled, invoiced, counted, stocked, marked up, insured, and financed many times before they are put into use. In the future, many of the steps in traditional retailing may be bypassed.

Consider, for example, a typical retailing system for the 1990s, made possible by modern systems of advertising, communications, and transportation. Each day a manufacturer of, say, video recorders buys cable television advertising time in a different city. Each evening, hundreds of consumers from that city call the toll-free number and place their orders, using credit cards for payment. That evening, as the machines roll off the assembly line at the factory in the Midwest, they are boxed, automatically labeled, and loaded into a UPS truck bound for the city, for delivery the next day. No warehouse or shopping mall ever sees the goods, no shelves are stocked, no cash register ever rings, and insurance and financing have been required for only 48 hours. The goods are cheaper, the consumer has his product without the necessity to visit a store, and the manufacturer has eliminated his finished inventory, while capturing much of the margin that once went to the wholesaler and the retailer.

● *The Automated Checkout Counter:* At the mall also, technology may lead to great productivity gains. Imagine, for example, a store checkout system in which the consumer inserts his bank card and then places the items he has selected on a conveyor belt leading to an automatic laser bar code reader. At the end of the belt, a specially adapted pick and place robot bags his items and hands the consumer his receipt. Except for stocking clerks, the self-service store has become fully automated.

EDUCATION: The productivity of the world's education systems has remained fundamentally unchanged since the days of Socrates. Teachers still stand in front of classes and deliver lectures to assembled groups of students. Learning per class hour or per teacher hour has shown little change in response to variations in the organization of school systems, teacher salaries, textbooks, or audiovisual aids.

The Computerized Classroom: Today's technology, if fully applied, could revolutionize education as dramatically as the automatic loom changed the textile industry. The classroom of the late 1990s could be a set of individual computer screens linked to massive information storage systems controlled by sophisticated software. The student would have instant electronic access to the best teachers, the most stimulating lessons, and the world's libraries of books, music, or film, assisted by teachers who are guides to the technology and the information sources rather than custodians of the knowledge. With individualized courses, self-paced instruction, and built-in testing, scoring, and evaluation of progress, the modern classroom could provide the equivalent of a personal tutor for each student. That part of education that involves the progressive mastery of large bodies of information could handled with far fewer lecturers, freeing teachers for the more challenging tasks of course design and development, leading group discussion or probing the limits of knowledge.

These examples of productivity possibilities in service industries could be repeated in many other areas. In protective services, for example, the potential to protect life or property with advanced sensing, detection, and monitoring systems has not been fully developed by either public or private security agencies. (Why, for example, do we have a large bureaucracy issuing traffic tickets and collecting tolls, when roadside sensors linked to computers could do the job for a fraction of the cost?) In the restaurant industry, the task of transmitting each patron's food order to the kitchen is still handled with the techniques and technology of two centuries ago, when a simple adaptation of a paging system could perform the job in much less time with many fewer errors. In financial services, the potential for home banking and electronic funds transfers—banking without tellers or loan officers, checks, deposit tickets and even cash—is still largely unexploited.

The Obstacles to Change

Of course, this brave new world filled with computer screens and automatic payments is threatening and even terrifying to many. Employees who fear job losses, consumers who resist buying automated services, and civil libertarians who fear government abuse of individual freedom must be convinced that the changes will benefit them. These fears have slowed the pace of change and the rate of productivity advance in many service industries and will continue to do so.

Indeed, the chief obstacles to productivity growth in services are not limits set by technology or the inherent nature of services but institutions and individuals who fear change. The lack of international competition in most services and the delivery of many of them by government monopolies have slowed change to a glacial pace. In most service institutions (with the obvious exception of retailing), there is the equivalent of the tenured faculty: a powerful group with no incentive to change. In the absence of a market to force action, this stand pat instinct usually prevails.

But there are signs that the barriers to change in many service industries may be about to fall. Many service industries that have been insulated from competition may be revolutionized in the not too distant future.

In health care, for example, the historic control of care by tradition-bound doctors reimbursed by third party payers is giving way to the development of HMOs, hospital chains, self-insured employers, and other large institutions with the incentive to deliver care in a cost-effective manner. These institutions will be motivated to improve productivity in ways that have not historically been given priority. The most innovative firms will begin to invest in more efficient management systems and in research and development of cost-saving technologies. Gradually, these investments will begin to create more efficient health-care systems.

In education, the government monopoly on elementary and secondary education is likely to remain largely intact for the foreseeable future, allowing these institutions to slow the pace of change. But the renewed emphasis on educational quality at the state level, and the proliferation of new approaches intended to achieve excellence in education, are laying the groundwork for significant changes in the years ahead. As these experiments are monitored and evaluated, the best practices and the successful technologies will receive more attention. As parents and politicians learn the results of the various programs, demands to apply the most successful systems and technologies will spread. Although these demands will not by themselves create a market in educational services, they will at least spur the public schools toward useful reforms.

At the same time, in the areas of training for the workplace, remedial education, and higher education, competition is likely to spur more rapid implementation of advanced technologies and much more rapid productivity gains. In these settings, where the institutional barriers to change are less dominant, and where emphasis on cost-effectiveness may be greater, innovations to promote efficiency are likely to catch on quickly. Successful methods proven outside the public schools will help to accelerate their adoption throughout the educational system.

In government, the continuing impact of deregulation at the federal level and the emerging trend toward privatization of state and local services may pay dividends in terms of more rapid adoption of new systems and technologies, and bigger boosts in productivity.

If the institutional resistance to change can be overcome, the technologies certainly exist to bring about spectacular improvements in the efficiency and productivity of the service industries, thereby substantially improving the income and well-being of the nation. After the long plateau in service industry productivity, the nation may be poised to enter a period of much more rapid gains.

Alternative Scenarios

Luck, unforeseen technological developments, or political and social shifts could all cause the economy to evolve much differently from the description painted in the baseline scenario. Policy choices could also change the future dramatically. To explore the impacts of major changes in policy, two alternative scenarios were developed.

The "deflation" scenario envisions a world in which policymakers turn inward and toward the past. In an attempt to preserve the old industries and traditional jobs, the United States veers toward protectionism. In fear of a repetition of the inflationary era of the 1970s, policy errs on the side of tight money and limited fiscal stimulus. And in a misunderstanding of the nature of the new economy, too little is invested in the development of human resources.

The "technology boom" scenario accelerates the most favorable technological and institutional changes of the baseline economy. It envisions rapid gains in service industry productivity, strong stimulus for worldwide demand, rapid growth of the developing countries in an open trading environment, and renewed interest in educating and training the workforce.

What would these different scenarios mean for jobs, economic growth, and labor markets in the U.S. over the next 13 years?

World Deflation: In the deflation scenario, the world tumbles into a vicious circle of slow growth from which it is unable to extricate itself. An initial recession against a backdrop of world trade imbalances triggers a spasm of trade restrictions by the United States. These in turn throw Japan and West Germany into recessions, which cause their imports of U.S. goods to fall, deepening U.S. economic problems. Although there is no tit-for-tat trade war, many nations begin to feel that they have been mistreated by their trading partners and implement policies aimed at securing a greater fraction of world exports. Coordination of economic policies breaks down, with the U.S. struggling to contain massive trade deficits, while West Germany and Japan timidly stimulate their weak economies. Many developing nations suffer severely, as their ability to export is weakened, and domestic and international confidence in their futures fades.

Although the world manages eventually to begin growing again, the severe damage to trading relations undermines confidence and causes growth to remain sluggish; two more recessions interrupt economic progress before the turn of the century.

As result of this environment, the world manages to grow by only 1.4 percent per year on average over the period, slightly worse than the 1.6 percent U.S. domestic rate. U.S. disposable income per person inches up only 0.6 percent per year, less than half the rate of the 1970–1985 period. With a surfeit of workers (unemployment averages 9 percent over the period), employers feel little need to invest, and productivity rises by only 0.7 percent per year. The only good news is that inflation is virtually eliminated, averaging less than half a percent per year. But even this silver lining is wrapped in a cloud, as it leads to historically high real interest rates, which cause severe problems for debt-strapped consumers and governments. Both the trade and budget deficits remain stuck at high levels, with a cumulative trade deficit over the period of $1.4 trillion and almost $2.3 trillion added to the federal debt.

The impacts of this grim scenario are instructive. Although protectionist policies are able to save about 830 thousand manufacturing jobs, they do so at a cost of more than 10 million service industry slots; moreover, manufacturing employment still declines, even though the rate is slower than under the baseline scenario. Although import growth virtually stops, exports grow by only 2 percent per year, so that the trade imbalance persists, and the cumulative current account deficit is some $500 billion greater than under the baseline scenario. Although the shift to services is arrested (the share of employment in manufacturing drops only to 15 percent in 2000, compared with 13 percent in the baseline scenario), wage gains fall far below those in the service-dominated baseline scenario.

In short, policies designed to preserve America's manufacturing base by limiting competition from foreign imports can slow down the restructuring of the nation's economy, but only at an enormous cost to the nation and the world.

Technology Boom: In contrast with the policies that promote a deflationary spiral in the slow-growth scenario, the technology boom scenario envisions a set of extraordinarily wise policy choices that trigger a stunning rebirth of American productivity and economic growth.

Recognizing the unusual opportunity presented by the slack in world commodity markets, world decisionmakers elect to boost worldwide demand boldly, and world GDP growth climbs by 3.6 percent per year. In the U.S., the prospect of tighter labor markets causes employers to invest heavily both in automation and in worker training, and, as a result, productivity rises by 2 percent per year. The gains are led by spectacular 4+ percent per year increases in manufacturing coupled with 1.6 percent average gains in services. Per capita disposable income grows by an impressive 2.7 percent per year—higher even than during the golden years from 1955 to 1970. Although inflation climbs back to nearly 4 percent, there is no return to double digits, and, as a result, real interest rates fall to about 3.5 percent. Unemployment falls slowly, but slips below 6 percent by the late 1990s.

The budget moves into surplus by 1995, and the cumulative deficit is some $400 billion less than under the baseline scenario. Although the current account deficit is slightly higher than under the baseline, due to the fact that the U.S. economy is growing faster than the world economy, U.S. exports climb at an alltime record pace of 6.7 percent per year, reaching $960 billion (in 1982 dollars) by the year 2000.

Again, the impacts of this scenario are instructive. Despite the accelerated shift to services (which accounts for some 81 percent of all employment by the year 2000 in this scenario), per capita incomes are some 20 percent above the baseline scenario and 40 percent above the protectionist world. Although government cuts back on intervention into international and domestic markets, it becomes more heavily involved in education and training, because it can afford to and because the returns justify doing so. As strong productivity and wage gains ease fears about foreign competition, there is increased lending to the developing nations. Their accelerating growth raises world growth rates and helps to stimulate the U.S. domestic economy. As years pass without a return of runaway price increases, the world begins to believe that it can indeed grow quickly without triggering inflation. Economic historians begin to write about the stagflation of the 1970s and early 1980s as an aberration from the long-term postwar trend.

The central lesson of these two alternative scenarios is that policies—wise and unwise—can make a difference. But strategies for holding back the pace of change and clinging to the industrial structure of a previous era have little chance of success and great likelihood of doing severe damage to the economy. On the other hand, the policies that appear to take risks by pushing the limits of growth, accelerating investment in human and physical capital, and removing the institutional barriers to productivity enhancements in services, can pay huge dividends.

CHAPTER 3
Work And Workers In The Year 2000

Who will be working in the year 2000 and what will they be doing? Which occupations will grow most rapidly? Which groups of workers will increase their presence in the workforce, and which will decline?

Many of these questions can be answered with some confidence. Everyone who will be working in the year 2000 has already been born, and two-thirds of them are at work today. Similarly, most of today's jobs will still exist in the year 2000. It is the new jobs and the new workers, however, that are of greatest interest and concern. The workers who will join the labor force between now and the year 2000 are not well-matched to the jobs that the economy is creating. A gap is emerging between the relatively low education and skills of new workers (many of whom are disadvantaged) and the advancing skill requirements of the new economy. Although this gap can certainly be bridged by education, training, automation, and other strategies, it presents a great challenge to American workers and employers. To understand the challenge, it is essential to review both detailed demographic projections and to forecast the occupational shifts ahead.

Demographics As Destiny—*WORKFORCE 2000*

Over the next 13 years, the American workforce and the economy will be shaped by five demographic "facts":

● *The population and the workforce will grow more slowly than at any time since the 1930s.*

● *The average age of the population and the workforce will rise, and the pool of young workers entering the labor market will shrink.*

• *More women will enter the workforce, although the rate of increase will taper off.*

• *Minorities will be a larger share of new entrants into the labor force.*

• *Immigrants will represent the largest share of the increase in the population and the workforce since the First World War.*

Slowly Growing Population

By the year 2000, the U.S. population will reach 275 million, an increase of 15 percent over the 240 million U.S. residents in 1985 (see Table 3-1).

This rate of gain, approximately one percent per year during the 1980s and three-fourths of one percent per year during the 1990s, is well below the average for the last two decades. By the 1990s, the U.S. population will be growing more slowly than at any time in the nation's history, with the exception of the decade of the Great Depression, when the rate was also about three-fourths of one percent per year (see Figure 3-1).

Changes in fertility, projected death rates, or immigration could have significant impacts on the size of the population over the next 15 years. For example, technological advances in birth control (a male contraceptive pill or a safe abortion-inducing drug) could sharply reduce the birth rate. Rapid advances in the treatment of cancer, or conversely, unchecked spread of the AIDS virus could alter the death rate. And changes in social values might encourage larger families among the affluent, as they did during earlier eras.

Under the most conservative assumptions (low fertility, high death rates, and low immigration), the population climbs to only

Table 3-1
U.S. POPULATION GROWTH, 1950–2000
(millions)

	Total	Increase Compared To Previous Census
1950	151.3	19.1
1960	179.3	28.0
1970	203.2	24.0
1980	226.5	23.2
1990	252.7	26.2
2000	275.2	22.5

Source: U.S. Bureau of the Census, Decennial Censuses and Current Population Reports, Series P-25, N. 937, Table 1, Hudson Institute.

Figure 3-1
POPULATION AND LABOR FORCE GROWTH WILL
DROP BY 2000
(Average Annual Gain)

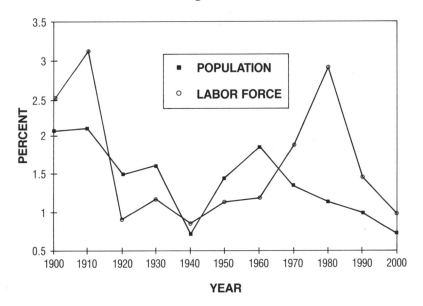

about 256 million, or seven percent. With opposite assumptions, the population could reach 281 million, a gain of 18 percent.

Changes in immigration represent the greatest uncertainties. The U.S. Bureau of the Census assumes that immigration during the balance of the century will match the rate of legal immigration during the recent past: 450,000 per year. At this rate, immigrants and their offspring will comprise a little more than one-fourth of the U.S. population gain. If immigration adds 750,000 persons per year to the population, i.e., if the estimated rate of legal and illegal immigration over the past 15 years continues unchanged, immigrants would account for almost half of the net gain.

Slower Labor Force Growth

The slowing growth of the population will be mirrored by the reduced growth of the labor force. Between 1985 and the year 2000, the labor force will grow by about 22 percent, from 115 million to 141 million (see Table 3-2).

Table 3-2
THE LABOR FORCE IS GROWING SLOWLY

Year	Labor Force	Gain From Previous Period
	(millions)	(millions)
1950	62.2	9.5
1960	69.6	7.4
1970	82.8	13.2
1980	106.9	24.1
1990	124.6	18.0
2000	140.5	15.6

Source: Bureau of Labor Statistics, Handbook of Labor Statistics, 1985, Table 4, and Hudson Institute.

Although the labor force gains are proportionally greater than the population gains (due to the increasing share of the population at work), the trend is the same: the labor force will be increasing at a slower rate than at any time since the 1930s (see Figure 3-1). Changes in birth and death rates could not significantly affect the size of the labor force during the balance of the century, since they would mostly affect children and old people who would not be working in any case. Immigration and changes in labor force participation, however, could have large impacts. For example, a strong economy could pull more workers into the labor market or international unrest could swell the numbers of illegal aliens seeking jobs. Conversely, a weak economy, growing desires for early retirement, renewed emphasis on child care by stay-at-home parents, or drastic border-closing legislation could all reduce the size of the labor force.

Combining the highest rates of immigration projected by the Census Bureau with the highest plausible rates of labor force participation projected by the Bureau of Labor Statistics would produce a labor force of 147 million in 2000. In contrast, the lowest projections would cause the labor force to rise to only 129 million. In other words, the workforce could increase by as little as 12 percent—the slowest rate in the country's history—or by as much as 28 percent—almost as fast as during the 1970s.

The Impacts of Slow Population and Labor Force Growth

The most likely scenario of slow population and labor force growth will affect the economy and the nation in a number of ways:

• *The national rate of economic growth will fall well below what it would be if the nation's population and workforce were increasing at the rates of the 1960s and 1970s.* Slower population growth will lead to less demand for population-sensitive products, such as food, automobiles, housing units, household goods, and educational services. Productivity gains will account for a much greater fraction of national growth than during the past two decades, when increases in population and workers helped to fuel the economy.

• *Economic growth will depend more directly on increased demand for income-sensitive products such as restaurant meals, luxury goods, travel, tourism, and health care.* Companies will focus more on capturing a larger share of disposable income, rather than on serving a greater share of households. As a result, services and luxury goods sectors of the economy will grow faster than population-dependent goods sectors.

• *Labor markets will be tighter, due to the slower growth of the workforce and the smaller reservoir of well-qualified workers.* While recessions may still lead to high unemployment, and undereducated workers may still suffer great difficulties in the labor market, fewer well-educated workers will be available than during the 1960s and 1970s, and employers may bid up their price.

An Aging Population and Workforce, and Fewer Young Workers

The aging of the baby boom generation (those born between 1946 and 1961) will cause the American population to become much older, on average, throughout the balance of the century. The median age of the population, which had been declining until 1970, will reach 36 by the year 2000, six years older than at any time in the history of the nation (see Figure 3-2).

Most of this aging will be the result of huge increases in the numbers of middle-aged Americans. Between 1986 and 2000, for example, the number of people between the ages 35–47 will jump by 38 percent, and the numbers age 48–53 will leap by a staggering 67 percent, compared with overall population growth of only 15 percent.

On the other hand, the population over age 65, which is sometimes assumed to be growing rapidly as part of the national aging trend, will actually grow more slowly for the balance of the

Figure 3-2
THE U.S. POPULATION IS GROWING OLDER
(Median Age)

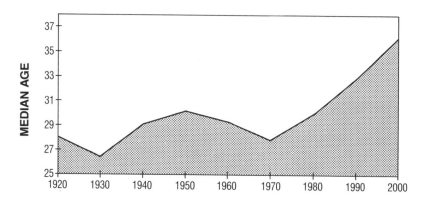

Source: U.S. Bureau of the Census, "Current Population
Reports," Series P-23, No. 138, Table 2-9

century than it has in recent years (see Table 3-3). Maturing, rather
than aging, may be the best description for the population trends of
the next decade and a half.

The number of young people will decline both relatively and
absolutely. The numbers between age 20 and 29, for example, will
shrink from 41 million in 1980 to 34 million in 2000, and their share of
the population will drop from 18 to 13 percent.

Table 3-3
THE POPULATION OVER AGE 65 WILL
GROW MORE SLOWLY, 1985–2000
(thousands, except percent)

	Total Over 65	Increase	Percent Increase
1950	12,397	X	X
1960	16,675	4,278	34.5
1970	20,087	3,412	20.5
1980	25,708	5,621	28.0
1990	31,680	5,972	23.2
2000	35,410	3,730	11.8

Source: U.S. Bureau of the Census, <u>Current Population Reports</u>, Series
P-23, No. 138, Table 2–1, Hudson Institute.

Figure 3-3
THE MIDDLE AGING OF THE WORKFORCE

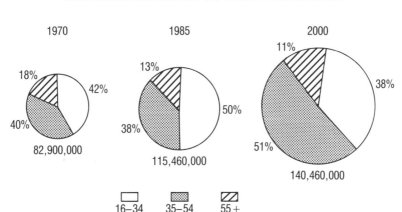

The age of the labor force will closely track the population, rising from a median of 35 years in 1984 to about 39 in 2000. All of the gains will come in the middle years of worklife, while the numbers at the two extremes decline. The number of workers age 35–54 will rise by more than 25 million, approximately equal to the total increase in the workforce (see Figure 3-3).

The Impacts of Aging

It is difficult to overestimate the impacts that this maturing of the population and the workforce will have on the society and the economy. While most commentary has focused on the benefits of an older workforce, the changes ahead will be both positive and negative, and the balance may be decidedly unfavorable. On the positive side:

● *A more experienced, stable, reliable, and generally healthy workforce should improve productivity.* The initial task of educating and training the huge baby boom generation has been largely accomplished; the investment in these workers should provide dividends to the economy over the next 13 years.

● *The economic dependency ratio (the proportion of the population not in the labor force compared to those in the labor force) will continue to drop.* This rough measure of the burden on the economy has been shrinking since the 1960s, with most of the reduction coming from the declining numbers of dependent children and nonworking wives. In 1965, for example, there were more than 1.5 dependents for each working person. By 1984, the ratio had dropped to 1.05 to one; in the year 2000, there will be less than one dependent per worker. Although this may enhance the nation's sense of well-being during the 1990s, it could lead to a false sense of security. Because the dependency ratio will turn around sharply when the baby boom retires after the turn of the century, the low numbers of dependents in the years to 2000 may postpone difficult political debates on issues such as Social Security funding. The healthy, working, middle-aged society of the 1990s may be reluctant to address the long-range costs of the retirement boom that will begin about 2010.

• *The national savings rate may rise, as the baby boomers reach middle age.* Younger people, who buy first houses, cars, and other consumer durables generally borrow more money than they save. Among those under age 35, net borrowing equals about 9 percent of income; between 35 and 44, families save about 3 percent of their incomes, while saving for those over 44 climbs to about 11 percent of their incomes. With the huge increase in the number of workers over age 40, higher national savings may lead to lower real interest rates, stimulating investment and improving productivity. In addition, the constituency opposing inflation may increase dramatically, as a much larger share of the population owns financial assets. Willingness to tolerate budget deficits or rapid monetary growth may decline. At the same time, tolerance for high unemployment as the price of a stable currency may increase.

• *Labor markets for younger workers could tighten.* Companies accustomed to hiring young workers at cheap wages may find that they must raise wages, reach further down the labor queue, invest in labor-saving technology, or all three, in order to prosper. Food service may be particularly affected.

On the other hand, the aging of the workforce may have some very negative consequences for the economy and the society:

• *The aging workforce may increase the rigidity of the economy.* An older, more stable workforce may adapt poorly to a rapidly-changing economy. For example, older people are much less likely to move than younger ones (see Figure 3-4). As the baby boomers reach the middle years of mortgages and children in school, their willingness to pull up stakes in response to new opportunities or changing conditions will decline. Similarly, the proportion of individuals who are

Figure 3-4
YOUNG PEOPLE ARE MUCH MORE LIKELY TO MOVE
(Inter-county Movers, 1976–1979)

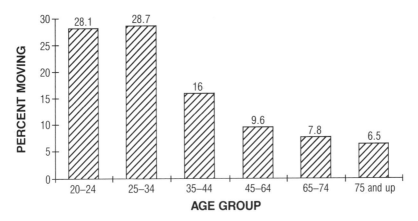

Source: U.S. Bureau of the Census, "Current Population Reports," Series P-23, No. 138, Table 4-6

willing to be retrained or who move between occupations declines steadily with age. For example, workers over age 45 were less than half as likely to change occupations between 1982 and 1983, compared with workers age 25 to 44 (see Figure 3-5).

• *The dearth of young workers may hamper the ability of companies to grow rapidly or to respond to change.* With the absolute numbers of new workers age 16–34 declining by almost 5 million, many companies may find themselves unable to move rapidly to hire large numbers of new workers to respond to changing economic conditions. The overnight creation of a Federal Express, an MCI, or an Apple Computer Company may become more difficult as the numbers of young people drop. The traditional process of "creative destruction," by which a company uses new hires to start a new division, while laying off older workers in slowly-growing sectors may become much more difficult. Not only will early retirements be more expensive, but wages of young workers may be higher. Impacts of this type will be felt most severely in the Midwest and Northeast, where outmigration over the last decade has dramatically reduced the numbers of current and future young workers. The North Central region of the country, for example, will experience a decline of three million people (22 percent) between the ages of 20 and 34 between 1980 and 2000, while the West experiences a gain of about one million (eight percent) at these ages.

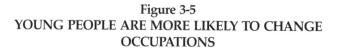

Figure 3-5
YOUNG PEOPLE ARE MORE LIKELY TO CHANGE OCCUPATIONS

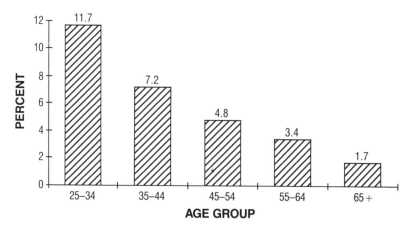

Source: "The Education, Training and Work Experience of the Adult Labor Force from 1984 to 1995," National Commission for Employment Policy, June 1985

● *Many companies with older workforces may find that their aging, higher-paid workers make them uncompetitive.* This will be particularly true of companies in slowly-growing industries or ones in which productivity is defined by production systems rather than by worker knowledge or skills, for example, automobiles, metals, and transportation. With no way to recover higher pay scales, higher pension charges (primarily as a result of vesting rather than actual retirements), and higher health care costs, companies may seek to roll back traditional seniority systems and other institutional arrangements for granting higher pay to older workers.

● *The job squeeze among middle-aged workers may become more intense.* The large increase in the numbers of middle-aged workers may collide with corporate efforts to reduce middle-management or to reduce vulnerability to demographic noncompetitiveness. Because a large fraction of the skills and productivity of older workers is valuable only to the firms they work for, older workers who lose jobs will have a particularly difficult time matching previous salaries when they find new jobs. A turbulent economy in which many firms are expanding and contracting in response to market conditions will be especially difficult for middle-aged and older workers. The long-standing pattern of increasing earnings until retirement may be substantially altered as a result.

• *Many industries that depend on young people for market growth will retrench.* Higher education, household furnishings, and rental housing construction could be most affected.

On balance, it appears that the impacts of the aging workforce may be favorable in the early 1990s, but could turn strongly negative by the turn of the century, as aging pushes the huge baby boom generation into its fifties.

Continued Feminization of the Workforce

Over the next 15 years, women are expected to continue to join the workforce in substantial numbers. By the year 2000, approximately 47 percent of the workforce will be women, and 61 percent of women will be at work. Women will comprise about three fifths of the new entrants into the labor force between 1985 and 2000 (see Table 3-4).

Much of the increase in the numbers of women in the labor force has come from increased participation by women with children. Of the 14.6 million married women who joined the labor force between 1960 an 1984, 8 million came from families with children. During that time period, the proportion of married mothers at work grew from 28 to 61 percent, and the share of all children under six whose mothers worked grew from 19 to 52 percent.

Women continue to be concentrated in traditionally female occupations that pay less than men's jobs. In 1980, 32 percent of all women were in jobs that were 90+ percent female, a figure that was

Table 3-4
WOMEN ARE GROWING SHARE OF THE WORKFORCE
(numbers in thousands, except percent)

	1950	1960	1970	1980	1990	2000
Women in the Workforce	18,389	23,240	31,543	45,487	57,230	66,670
Female Labor Force Participation Rate	33.9	37.7	43.3	51.5	57.5	61.1
Female Share of The Workforce	29.6	33.4	38.1	42.5	45.8	47.5

Source: U.S. Bureau of Labor Statics, <u>Handbook of Labor Statistics, 1985</u>, Tables 4 and 5; and unpublished data.

Figure 3-6
WOMEN HOLD A GROWING SHARE OF MANAGERIAL
AND PROFESSIONAL JOBS
(Percent Female)

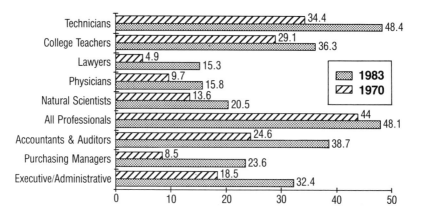

Source: U.S. Bureau of the Census, 1980 Census of the
Population, Supplementary Reports; and Bureau of Labor
Statistics, "Handbook of Labor Statistics, 1985, Table 18

little changed from the 28 percent in 90+ female jobs in 1960. And in
1983, the wages of women working full-time were only 66 percent
those of men, up only 4 percentage points from the figure in 1967.

There are signs however, that these patterns may change substantially over the next 13 years. For example, women are a rapidly
increasing share of many traditionally male occupations, particularly
those requiring advanced education (see Figure 3-6).

These proportions are likely to rise further over the next 15 years,
as the number of women graduating from professional schools
increases. For example, in 1983, 45 percent of those receiving accounting degrees, 36 percent of new lawyers, 36 percent of computer
science majors, and 42 percent of business majors were women. And
although women's wages relative to men's have shown little improvement when looked at over two decades, the pattern of the last five
years is more encouraging, with relative wages gaining five percentage points in five years. One Rand study projects that women's
wages will equal 74 percent of men's by the year 2000.

The flood of women entering the workforce during the last three
decades has been driven by powerful social and economic trends.

Slow economic growth has made two earners a necessity for many families striving for a middle class lifestyle. Technology has simplified homemaking at the same time that society has redefined the role of women to include paid employment as the norm for most.

At least two facts, however, suggest that the entrance of women into the workforce will slow down and may peak by the year 2000:

• *Labor force participation rates for women aged 55–64 peaked in 1969 and are now two percentage points below their high.* As more women are able to retire early on their own or their husband's pensions, labor force participation among this group may decline. If labor force participation among this age group were to maintain its 15-year downtrend, about 500,000 fewer women would be in the labor force in the year 2000 than are currently projected by the Bureau of Labor Statistics.

• *Mothers want to work less than they do now.* According to a recent Gallup poll, only 13 percent of working women with children want to work full-time, regular hours, although 52 percent of them hold full-time jobs. Six of ten working mothers want part-time employment, flexible hours, or stay-at-home jobs, and 16 percent would prefer not to work at all. Only half of all women believe that they can adequately fulfil their responsibilities to their children if they work full-time. If employers fail to provide sufficient jobs with flexible working arrangements, more mothers may choose to leave the labor force during their child-rearing years, further reducing the numbers of new workers entering the workforce.

The Impact of Working Women

Even if rates of female labor force participation rise more slowly than projected, the impacts of the increased numbers of women in the workforce will still be profound. In less than a generation, the nation's pattern of employment has been radically altered, from one in which most married women stayed home, to one in which nearly everyone is paid to work. Because so much of the change has occurred since 1960, the society has not fully digested its implications. Over the next 13 years, policies and patterns of child rearing, taxation, pensions, hiring, compensation, and industrial structure will change to conform to the new realities:

• *The economic growth that the economy has enjoyed as a result of the shift of women from low-productivity, unpaid housework to paid employment will taper off.* Between 1970 and 1980, 14 million women joined the

workforce; between 1990 and 2000, only 9 million will do so. As fewer
women move from the unmeasured to the measured economy,
economic growth rates will be lower.

- *Day care and pre-school education will become more heavily subsidized,
  institutionalized, and regulated.* Parents, government, and industry will
  all become more involved. As evidence accumulates concerning the
  positive impacts on children of high-quality day care, the pressure for
  ever higher standards will grow. Day care, like health care during the
  1970s, will claim a rising fraction of national income. By the year 2000,
  it may be routine for employers to subsidize or directly provide care,
  and school systems may have lowered the age for starting school to
  five or younger. Federal day care programs for children of welfare
  mothers, early childhood education for disadvantaged children, and
  tax subsidies for child care may be substantially expanded.

- *The tax system will be subject to periodic readjustments of the "marriage
  penalty," child care deductions, and other anomalies,* as society struggles to
  reconcile its notions of fairness and its desire to promote families,
  with the reality of higher incomes for two-earner families.

- *The workforce may become less flexible, as two-career families become less
  willing to move.* Although corporations will be forced to provide more
  relocation assistance to spouses, the two-career trend will reinforce
  the rigidity that develops because of aging. Middle aged, two-career
  families will become geographically immobile.

- *The distinctions between male and female jobs and wage rates will decline
  in response to market pressures, and possibly as a result of union and
  government intervention.* The rapid rate at which women are being
  integrated into the professions will make sex discrimination less of a
  concern by the year 2000 than it is today.

- *Part-time, flexible, and stay-at-home jobs will increase, and total work
  hours per employee are likely to drop in response to the needs of women to
  integrate work and child-rearing.* In combination with the continued
  trend toward early retirement, a greater fraction of national income
  will be taken as leisure, and this will depress measured GNP.

- *Benefit policies are likely to be restructured to reflect the desires of
  two-earner families and single workers.* For example, "cafeteria" benefit
  plans, which enable a worker to choose from a menu of health,
  retirement, leave, and other benefits, subject only to a dollar limita-
  tion, are likely to become more widespread. Under such plans, a

single parent might choose more day care, health, and flexible leave options, while a middle-aged household head might choose more insurance, retirement, or savings programs. Similarly, private pension benefits are likely to be tied more closely to individuals and their earnings, and to be based less on years of service, family status, and income from other sources such as Social Security.

● *In contrast to this tailoring of private plans to individual needs and earnings, public programs are likely to move in the other direction*, with a trend towards increased means-testing of social security, Medicare, and federal pensions, and increased support for families with children. As a result of these diverging patterns, society's access to many pension, health, and other benefits is likely to be increasingly segregated between those available to earners—which are strictly tied to economic value, and those available through government—which are increasingly oriented toward individuals with lower income and children.

Minorities Will Be A Growing Share of the Workforce

Over the next 13 years, blacks, Hispanics, and other minorities will make up a large share of the expansion of the labor force. Non-whites, for example, will comprise 29 percent of the net additions to the workforce between 1985 and 2000 and will be more than 15 percent of the workforce in the year 2000 (see Table 3-5).

Black women will comprise the largest share of the increase in the non-white labor force. In fact, by the year 2000, black women will outnumber black men in the workforce, a striking contrast to the pattern among whites, where men outnumber women by almost three to two.

Table 3–5
NON-WHITES ARE A GROWING SHARE
OF THE WORKFORCE
(numbers in millions)

	1970	1985	2000
Working Age Population (16+)	137.1	184.1	213.7
Non-White Share	10.9%	13.6%	15.7%
Labor Force	82.8	115.5	140.4
Non-White Share	11.1%	13.1%	15.5%
Labor Force Increase (Over Previous Period)	X	32.7	25.0
Non-White Share	X	18.4%	29.0%

Source: Bureau of Labor Statistics, <u>Handbook of Labor Statistics, 1985</u>, Table 4 and 5; and Hudson Institute.

Table 3-6
BLACKS AND HISPANICS ARE MUCH LESS
SUCCESSFUL IN THE LABOR MARKKET
(1983)

	White	Black	Hispanic
Labor Force Participation	64.3	61.5	63.8
Unemployment Rate	8.4	19.5	13.7
Median Family Employment (Weekly)	$487	$348	$366
Percent Below Poverty	12.1	35.7	28.4
Median Years of Schooling	12.8	12.5	12.1

Source: U.S. Bureau of Labor Statistics, U.S. Bureau of the Census.

By almost every measure of employment, labor force participation, earnings, and education, black and Hispanic minorities suffer much greater disadvantages than whites (see Table 3-6).

To these statistical indices must be added the extensively analyzed and debated indications of social disadvantage, such as poor performance in schools, greater dependence on welfare, greater incidence of broken families and children born to unmarried mothers, and higher rates of criminal arrest.

Two particularly disturbing trends in the patterns of disadvantage among minorities are the declines in male labor force participation and the related increase in the numbers of female household heads. From 1970 to 1984, for example, the proportion of prime age black men in the labor force dropped from 79 percent to 74 percent, while the proportion of black families headed by women rose from 28 to 43 percent.

The Uncertain Outlook

Though it appears very likely that the labor market will be increasingly comprised of disadvantaged minorities over the next 13 years, it is much less clear whether the disadvantages these groups suffer will be getting better or worse during this period of tighter labor markets. Several factors are worth noting:

• *Relative rates of unemployment and earnings have not improved during the past decade and may be becoming worse.* For example, the ratio of black family income to white family income, which rose from .54 to .61 between 1950 and 1970, fell back to .56 in 1983. For Hispanics, family income figures show a drop from .71 to .66 between 1973 and 1983. Black unemployment, which averaged about 2.1 times white rates from 1972 to 1977, climbed to 2.4 times white rates from 1978 to 1983. For Hispanics, the ratio was stable at about 1.6.

- *Blacks and Hispanics are overrepresented among declining occupations.* In a study by the Equal Employment Opportunity Commission, both groups were 35 percent more likely to be employed in occupations projected by the BLS to lose the most employees between 1978 and 1990.
- *Blacks and Hispanics are concentrated in a small number of central cities beset by severe problems.* Fifty-seven percent of blacks and 49 percent of Hispanics, compared to 25 percent of whites, live in central cities. Forty percent of all blacks live in 11 cities, only two of which, Los Angeles and Atlanta, are in the highest growth regions of the country.

The prospect that minorities will comprise a very large fraction of the new additions to the labor force over the next 13 years appears, on the surface, to present an unprecedented opportunity. As employers reach further down the labor queue, they might be expected to provide better job prospects for historically disadvantaged groups and to invest more heavily in their education and training.

But the pattern of job growth in higher-technology occupations requiring more education, and the likelihood of greater employment gains in metropolitan regions with fewer minority residents, suggest that this sanguine outlook is far from assured. In fact, given the historic patterns of behavior by employers, it is more reasonable to expect that they will bid up the wages of the relatively smaller numbers of white labor force entrants, seek to substitute capital for labor in many service occupations, and/or move job sites to the faster growing, more youthful parts of the country, or perhaps of the world. Blacks, and particularly black men, are those most likely to be put at risk if such strategies dominate.

Immigrants Will Be a Growing Share of the Population and the Labor Force

Between 1970 and 1980, the foreign-born population of the U.S. (as counted by the Census Bureau) grew by about 4.5 million, accounting for about a fifth of the U.S. population gain during the period. While this number was more than a third greater than the number who entered in the 1960s, it was small by historical standards. At the turn of the century, for example, immigrants added about one percent per year to the U.S. population, compared with the current rate of about one-fifth of one percent.

In the wake of amendments to the immigration laws in 1965, recent immigrants have come mostly from Latin America and Asia, in dramatic contrast to earlier immigrants. Of those who entered the country after 1970, 78 percent came from these two regions; of those entering the country before 1960, 79 percent came from Canada and Europe.

Most of the new immigrants have settled in the South and West. The number of foreign-born residents in the South grew by 120 percent from 1970 to 1980, and by 97 percent in the West. In the North and Midwest, the numbers increased by only 10 percent. Three states, California, Texas, and New York, account for more than half of all foreign-born residents. One-fifth of all recent immigrants live in the Los Angeles area.

Immigrants represent a broad spectrum of social and educational backgrounds. Of adults who entered the U.S. in the 1970s, 25 percent had less than five years of school, compared to three percent of native-born Americans; on the other hand, 22 percent were college graduates, compared with 16 percent of natives.

Estimates of net inflow of illegal aliens into the country vary widely. The most recent Census Bureau estimates suggest that the number of illegals residing in the U.S. may be between 4 and 6 million, and the Council of Economic Advisors has estimated that this figure was increasing by between 100,000 and 300,000 people per year through the mid-1980s.

A number of factors suggest that, in the absence of radical policy changes, the number of legal and illegal immigrants will continue to be substantial. As the preferred destination for those seeking economic opportunity or political refuge, the U.S. will remain a powerful magnet for the rapidly-growing populations of Latin America and Asia. Between 1985 and 2000, for example, the population of Latin America alone is expected to increase by 150 million people.

Recent legislation that imposes sanctions against employers of illegal aliens may reduce this economic attraction. But the experience of other countries such as France, Canada, Switzerland, and West Germany that have imposed employer sanctions indicates that they are ineffective in controlling immigration, without vigorous enforcement. Moreover, legal immigration, which is a matter of right to members of the immediate family of naturalized citizens, is sure to increase simply as a result of the echo effect of the recent increases in legal immigration, as well as the legalization provisions of the new immigration law. As more recent immigrants become citizens, they will be entitled to bring in spouses and children without quota limitations.

For these reasons, if the conditions of the 1970s and early 1980s do not change radically, at least 450,000 immigrants are likely to enter the U.S. each year for the balance of the century. Immigration at this rate would add about 9.5 million people to the U.S. population (including the children of immigrants) and approximately 4 million to the U.S. labor force. If illegal immigration continues at recent rates, and legal immigration is unchanged, the 750,000 annual immigrants will swell the population by 16.1 million and the labor force by 6.8 million. A mid-point forecast of 600,000 immigrants annually is used in the surprise-free scenario. Even under the most conservative assumptions, both the Hispanic and Asian populations are likely to double, to 30 million and 10 million, by the year 2000. As they have in the past, most of these new residents will cluster in the cities and states where they are concentrated today. California is likely to be particularly affected, with more than two-fifths of its population being Hispanic or Asian by the year 2000.

The Impacts of Immigration

Although immigration triggers fears of job losses and earnings stagnation, the evidence suggests that, on balance, levels of immigration of 450,000–750,000 will benefit the country. For example, studies of the Los Angeles labor market, where more than 1 million foreign-born persons settled during the 1970s, show that job growth was well above the national average during the period and that unemployment fell below national rates. Although manufacturing wages were depressed as a result of the immigrant influx, service industry wages, in which native-born American were concentrated, rose faster than the national average.

Since immigrants to Los Angeles have been both less-educated (57 percent had less than a grade school education) and more numerous than those expected nationally over the next 13 years, the Los Angeles experience is a persuasive argument that immigration need not overwhelm the "carrying capacity" of the country.

One particularly important concern with immigration is its impact on the job prospects of native minorities. Although the evidence is not definitive, the results of one statistical analysis of 247 metropolitan areas concluded that black unemployment rates are not increased by a rise in the proportion of Mexican immigrants in a local labor market. These results suggest that, to some extent, immigrants are complementary to, rather than in competition with, native minority workers.

In fact, it is plausible that residents of areas that experience significant influxes of immigrants will benefit rather than suffer from the new workers. This will be particularly likely over the long-run. Census data and other studies have shown that, over 10 or 20 years, the earnings of immigrants and their offspring will equal or exceed those of native-born Americans with similar characteristics. The South and West, already enriched by their comparative surfeit of young workers, will be even more likely to attract new jobs and self-reinforcing economic growth, if immigration rises and if these immigrants succeed in the labor market in later years.

Despite the evidence of economic benefits, immigration has always triggered negative emotional reactions from natives, and the current concerns with the "loss of control" of U.S. borders are continuing this tradition. A plurality of poll respondents favor less immigration, and only 7 percent favor more. It is not unlikely that, over the next 13 years, the political reaction to these voter attitudes will lead to much more restrictive and vigorously-enforced legislation and to dramatically reduced immigration flows.

One particularly ominous version of this scenario might result from an explosive increase in the numbers of immigrants following, for example, a major revolution in Central or South America. Huge numbers of refugees might throng into the country, followed by the passage of harsh laws and strict border controls. The supply of immigrant labor might become one more rapidly-fluctuating factor in the economic equation of the South and West, similar to the price of oil, the value of the dollar, or the rate of inflation.

Even if no radical border-closing laws are passed, one likely outcome of the anti-immigrant emotions will be greater divisions between Hispanics and blacks. If the labor market experience of Hispanics and blacks diverges, the unity of interest that currently appears to unite these groups may crumble. By the year 2000, it is possible that the political relationships between blacks and Hispanics will be beginning to resemble those between blacks and older urban ethnic groups such as the Italians, Irish, or Poles.

Figure 3-7
MOST NEW ENTRANTS TO THE LABOR FORCE WILL
BE NON-WHITE, FEMALE OR IMMIGRANTS

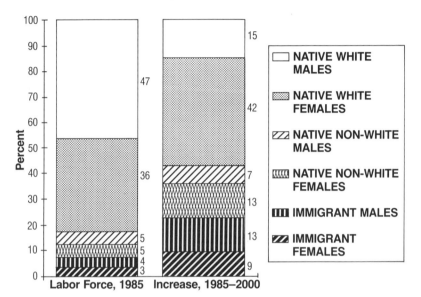

Source: Hudson Institute

The Workforce of 2000

The cumulative impact of the changing ethnic and racial composition of the labor force will be dramatic. The small net growth of workers will be dominated by women, blacks, and immigrants. White males, thought of only a generation ago as the mainstays of the economy, will comprise only 15 percent of the net additions to the labor force between 1985 and 2000 (see Figure 3-7).

For companies that have previously hired mostly young white men, the years ahead will require major changes. Organizations from the military services to the trucking industry will be forced to look beyond their traditional sources of personnel. For well-qualified minorities and women, the opportunities will be unusually great.

The Changing Job Mix

What will be workforce of 2000 be doing? The changes projected for the nation's industrial structure will restructure U.S. occupational patterns. The jobs that will be created between 1987 and 2000 will be substantially different from those in existence today. A number of jobs in the least-skilled job classes will disappear, while high-skilled professions will grow rapidly. Overall, the skill mix of the economy will be moving rapidly upscale, with most new jobs demanding more education and higher levels of language, math, and reasoning skills. These occupational changes will present a difficult challenge for the disadvantaged, particularly for black men and Hispanics, who are underrepresented in the fastest growing professions and overrepresented in the shrinking job categories.

Predicting The Jobs of the Future

Each industry requires a different mix of occupations to create its products or services. The insurance industry, for example, requires far more accountants and lawyers and many fewer cashiers than the retailing business. Within manufacturing, research-intensive industries such as computers require more scientists and engineers, but employ fewer tool and die makers than traditional industries such as steel or automobiles.

The occupational mix of each industry changes gradually, as industries adjust to their evolving environment by employing people with different skills and occupational titles. The health-care industry, for example, is increasingly dominated by large national firms that manage a wide variety of hospitals, clinics, and other facilities. For this reason, the industry is employing increasing numbers of managers and administrators whose jobs did not exist 15 years ago.

By projecting these changes in the mix of occupations in each industry and applying the projected matrix to the predicted industrial structure of the economy in the year 2000, it is possible to forecast coming changes in the mix of occupations.[2] The results suggest that the job prospects for professional and technical, managerial, sales, and service jobs will far outstrip the opportunities in other fields. In contrast to the average gain of about 25 percent across all occupational categories, the fastest growing fields—lawyers, scientists, and health profession-

---

[2]See the technical appendix for details of the methodology employed in these projections.

Table 3-7

THE CHANGING OCCUPATIONAL STRUCTURE, 1984–2000

Occupation	Current Jobs (000s)	New Jobs (000s)	Rate of Growth (Percentage)
Total	105,008	25,952	25
Service Occupations	16,059	5,957	37
Managerial and Management-Related	10,893	4,280	39
Marketing and Sales	10,656	4,150	39
Administrative Support	18,483	3,620	20
Technicians	3,146	1,389	44
Health Diagnosing and Treating Occupations	2,478	1,384	53
Teachers, Librarians, and Counselors	4,437	1,381	31
Mechanics, Installers, and Repairers	4,264	966	23
Transportation and Heavy Equipment Operators	4,604	752	16
Engineers, Architects, and Surveyors	1,447	600	41
Construction Trades	3,127	595	19
Natural, Computer, and Mathematical Scientists	647	442	68
Writers, Artists, Entertainers, and Athletes	1,092	425	39
Other Professionals and Paraprofessionals	825	355	43
Lawyers and Judges	457	326	71
Social, Recreational, and Religious Workers	759	235	31
Helpers and Laborers	4,168	205	5
Social Scientists	173	70	40
Precision Production Workers	2,790	61	2
Plant and System Workers	275	36	13
Blue Collar Supervisors	1,442	−6	0
Miners	175	−28	−16
Hand Wworkers, Assemblers, and Fabricators	2,604	−179	−7
Machine Setters, Operators, and Tenders	5,527	−448	−8
Agriculture, Forestry, and Fisheries	4,480	−538	−12

Source: Hudson Institute.

als—will grow two to three times as fast. On the other hand, jobs as machine tenders, assemblers, miners, and farmers actually decline (see Table 3-7).

Rising Educational and Skill Requirements

Among the fastest-growing jobs, the trend toward higher educational requirements is striking. Of all the new jobs that will be created over the 1984–2000 period, more than half will require some education beyond high school, and almost a third will be filled by college graduates. Today, only 22 percent of all occupations require a college degree. The median years of education required by the new jobs created between 1984 and 2000 will be 13.5, compared to 12.8 for

Table 3-8
THE OCCUPATIONS OF THE FUTURE WILL REQUIRE MORE
EDUCATION

	Current Jobs	New Jobs
Total	100%	100%
8 Years or Less	6%	4%
1–3 Years of High School	12%	10%
4 Years of High School	40%	35%
1–3 Years of College	20%	22%
4 Years of College or More	22%	30%
Median Years of School	12.8	13.5

Source: Bureau of Labor Statistics, Hudson Institute.

the current workforce (see Table 3-8).

Looked at another way, of the job categories listed in Table 3-7 that are growing faster than average, all but one—service occupations—require more than the median level of education for all jobs. Of those growing slowly or declining, not one requires more than the median education (see Figure 3-8).

These estimates assume that, for each occupation, the new jobs created will require the same levels of education required for that occupation today. The recent trend, however, is toward higher education levels in each job category. If this trend prevails, levels of educational attainment required for new jobs may be even higher than those projected.

Education levels, of course, are only a rough proxy for the skills required for employment. But more detailed analysis of the language, math, and reasoning skills required for various jobs reinforces the conclusion that the skill mix of the U.S. economy will rise substantially between now and the end of the century. For example, when occupations are ranked by the U.S. Department of Labor according to a specific set of skill criteria, there is a direct correlation between the level of skills required and the rate of growth of employment in the occupation. Ranking of all jobs according to the skills required on a scale of 1–6, with six being the highest level of skills,[3] indicates that

---

[3]For example, in the area of language development, a job rated 6 might require an individual to read literature or scientific and technical publications, and to write journals or speeches. A level 2 might require only the ability to read stories and simple instructions, write compound and complex sentences, and speak using all tenses. In math, the top-skill group would be expected to use advanced calculus, econometrics, or statistical probabilities, while a level 2 would be expected only to add, subtract, multiply, and divide, compute ratios and percents, and interpret bar graphs. See the technical appendix for more details.

Table 3-9
FAST-GROWING JOBS REQUIRE MORE LANGUAGE, MATH, AND REASONING SKILLS

	Current Jobs	Fast Growing	Slowly Growing	Declining
Language Rating	3.1	3.8	2.7	1.9
Math Rating	2.6	3.1	2.3	1.6
Reading Rating	3.5	4.2	3.2	2.6

Source: Hudson Institute.

the fastest-growing jobs require much higher math, language, and reasoning capabilities than current jobs, while slowly-growing jobs require less. Natural scientists and lawyers, for example, whose average skill requirements are the highest rated at 5.7 and 5.2, are also the two fastest-growing occupations, with each field slated to add up to 70 percent more workers. Occupations in decline, on the other hand, show some of the lowest levels of required skill.(see Table 3-9) For example, machine setters and hand working occupations have language skill ratings of 1.8 and 1.7, and both will decline by more than 7 percent by the year 2000.

Looked at in aggregate, the picture is even starker. When skill requirements in language, reasoning, and mathematics are averaged, only four percent of the new jobs can be filled by individuals with the lowest levels of skills, compared to 9 percent of jobs requiring such low skills today. At the other end of the scale, 41 percent of the new jobs will require skills ranked in one of the top three categories, compared with only 24 percent that require such proficiency at present (see Figure 3-8).

Although the overall pattern of job growth is weighted toward higher-skilled occupations, very large numbers of jobs will be created in some medium-to low-skilled fields. In absolute numbers, the biggest job creation categories will be service occupations, administrative support, and marketing and sales, which together account for half of the net new jobs that will be created. In the service category, the largest groups are cooks, nursing aides, waiters, and janitors. Among administrative support jobs, secretaries, clerks, and computer operators predominate. In marketing and sales, most of the new slots will be for cashiers. With the exception of computer operators, most of these large categories require only modest levels of skill.

But even for these jobs, whose typical skill scores fall in the middle of the current skill range with total scores between 2.5 and 3,

Figure 3-8
LOW SKILLED JOBS ARE DECLINING

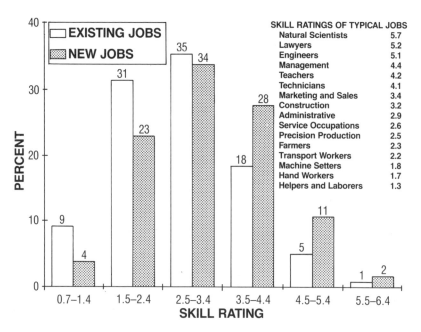

Source: Hudson Institute.

workers will be expected to read and understand directions, add and subtract, and be able to speak and think clearly. In other words, jobs that are currently in the middle of the skill distribution will be the least-skilled occupations of the future, and there will be very few net new jobs for the unskilled.

Moreover, these middle/low-skilled jobs are concentrated in service industries in which wage gains and productivity growth have traditionally been weak. Over the past two decades, a self-reinforcing pattern of job growth for low-skilled, low-productivity, low-paid workers has dominated much of the service economy. This has been a two-edged sword. On the one hand, it has provided millions of jobs for relatively low-skilled workers. On the other, it has hampered the improvement of productivity in the economy and held down overall wage gains.

As discussed earlier, demographic, institutional, and technological changes are likely to force substantial streamlining and automation of many service industries by the year 2000. When this occurs, it will benefit the economy by raising overall productivity and wage levels within these industries. For unskilled workers, however, it will mean that job opportunities may be even scarcer than these projections suggest. Unless the nation is able to bring even its least able workers up to higher standards of education and skills, it is likely that average rates of unemployment will rise, as service industries are automated. If service industry productivity rises as expected, the pattern of structural unemployment at ever-higher levels during each cyclical recovery will become more pronounced.

The Impact of the Changing Job Market On Minority Workers

How will the changing job market affect the employment prospects of the various groups within the society? In particular, what do the changes promise for disadvantaged groups such as blacks and Hispanics?

By analyzing the current occupational patterns of blacks, Hispanics, and others, and projecting these patterns onto the occupational matrix forecast for the year 2000, it is possible to estimate the likely impacts of the changing job market. If each group is assumed to retain its share of the jobs in each occupational category, the overall impact of the changing job market on the job prospects of various groups of workers can be estimated. Comparing this implied job share with the projections of the share of the new labor force entrants that various groups will comprise gives an indication of the degree to which traditional occupational patterns must change over the next decade and a half. Although such an analysis should not be interpreted as a projection, it can indicate the scale of the challenge that the society faces in fully employing all its members in the future.

For black men and Hispanics, the job market will be particularly difficult (see Table 3-10). In contrast to their rising share of the new entrants into the labor force, black men will hold a *declining* fraction of all jobs if they simply retain existing shares of various occupations. Black women, on the other hand, will hold a rising fraction of all jobs if they retain their current shares of each occupation, but this increase will be less than needed to offset their growing share of the workforce.

Similarly, although the economy will be creating more jobs in the categories traditionally held by middle-aged workers and women, the increases will not be enough to offset the increases in the labor force

Table 3-10
BLACK MEN AND HISPANICS FACE THE GREATEST
DIFFICULTIES IN THE EMERGING JOB MARKET

Group	Share of Current Jobs	Implied Share of New Jobs (1985–2000)	Share of Labor Force Growth
Women	45.0%	50.5%	59.3%
Blacks	9.9%	9.5%	19.7%
Black Men	4.9%	3.8%	7.7%
Black Women	5.1%	5.6%	12.0%
Hispanics	6.4%	5.0%	22.0%
Ages 16–24	19.1%	17.9%	−9.6%
25–44	51.6%	53.0%	44.8%
45+	29.3%	29.1%	64.8%

Source: Hudson Institute Projections.

in these categories. For young people, the small decline in the numbers of jobs they traditionally have held will be overwhelmed by a large decline in the numbers of young people entering the workforce. This suggests both that there will be substantial shifts in sex/race/age distribution of various occupations and that the greatest shifts must be made by minorities and by older workers and females. But because minorities are currently the least advantaged in terms of their skill levels and educational backgrounds, the transition for them will be particularly difficult.

The Implications of the Changing Occupational Structure

This rapid increase in the skills required for new jobs in the economy must be put in the context of the competence of the new workers entering the workforce. The evidence suggests that many millions of these new workers lack even the basic skills essential for employment. For example, the recent National Assessment of Educational Progress undertaken by the U.S. Department of Education (NAEP) found that among 21–25 year olds:

—only about three-fifths of whites, two-fifths of Hispanics, and a quarter of blacks could locate information in a news article or an almanac;

—only a quarter of whites, 7 percent of Hispanics, and 3 percent of blacks could decipher a bus schedule;

—only 44 percent of whites, 20 percent of Hispanics, and 8 percent of blacks could correctly determine the change they were due from the purchase of a two-item restaurant meal.

The forces that are shaping the U.S. economy will make it increasingly difficult for young Americans such as these to succeed in the job market. In particular, as change accelerates and more training is needed, many workers will need advanced skills simply to give them access to useful job training. For example, assembly-line workers in many manufacturing plants are learning statistical process control, a system that is beyond the reach of those without a solid grounding in mathematics.

As the U.S. economy becomes increasingly integrated with the world economy, the ability of the U.S. government or American unions to insulate workers without skills from competition with unskilled workers in other countries will decline. A decade ago, it was possible to pay unskilled janitors in automobile plants $12 per hour, because they worked in unionized, high-productivity plants in a wealthy economy. The economy of the future will not produce or sustain such high-wage, low-skill jobs.

During the 1985–2000 period, the good fortune to be born in or to immigrate to the United States will make less difference than the luck or initiative to be well-educated and well-trained. For individuals, the good jobs of the future will belong to those who have skills that enable them to be productive in a high-skill, service economy. For the nation, the success with which the workforce is prepared for high-skilled jobs will be an essential ingredient in maintaining a high-productivity, high-wage economy.

CHAPTER 4
Six Challenges

Most of the laws and policies that affect American jobs and workers were developed several decades ago. Many date from the 1930s and 1960s, when economic conditions were different, world trade was less important, manufacturing was more dominant, and women and minorities were a smaller share of the workforce. As the changes in the American economy and workforce unfold over the balance of the century, many of these policies will become increasingly outmoded. Between now and the year 2000, six issues will require rethinking and revision:

● *Stimulating Balanced World Growth:* The U.S. must pay less attention to its share of world trade and more to the growth of the economies of the other nations of the world, including those nations in Europe, Latin America, and Asia with whom the U.S. competes.

● *Accelerating Productivity Increases in Service Industries:* Prosperity will depend much more on how fast output per worker increases in health care, education, retailing, government, and other services, than on gains in manufacturing.

● *Maintaining the Dynamism of an Aging Workforce:* As the average age of American workers climbs toward 40, the nation must insure that its workforce does not lose its adaptability and willingness to learn.

● *Reconciling the Conflicting Needs of Women, Work, and Families:* Despite the huge increases in the numbers of women in the workforce, many of the policies and institutions that cover pay, fringe benefits, time away from work, pensions, welfare, and other issues have not yet been adjusted to the new realities.

● *Integrating Black and Hispanic Workers Fully Into the Economy:* The shrinking numbers of young people, the rapid pace of industrial change, and the rising skill requirements of the emerging economy make the task of fully utilizing minority workers particularly urgent between now and 2000.

- *Improving the Education and Skills of All Workers:* Human capital—knowledge, skills, organization, and leadership—is the key to economic growth and competitiveness.

Stimulating World Growth

For more than a decade, American policymakers have been concerned with the U.S. balance of trade, the nation's deteriorating ability to compete internationally, and the presumed unfairness of the trading policies of other countries. These are not unimportant issues. They are not, however, the most critical international problems facing the nation.

U.S. prosperity between now and the end of the century will depend primarily on how fast the world economy grows and on how rapidly domestic productivity increases. It will depend very little on how open or closed the Japanese market is to American goods or even on how soon U.S. trade accounts return to balance.

A historical analogy clarifies the point. Almost a century ago, Michigan and Indiana were both production sites for automobiles, and companies in the two states competed aggressively for markets. By the second decade of the twentieth century, however, the battle was over, and Michigan had emerged as the primary location of this important industry. Over the next five decades, enormous wealth was created in Michigan, as the rest of the nation bought millions of these expensive consumer products.

But the Hoosiers did not become poor as Michigan became rich. Instead, the vast wealth created in Michigan created new markets for thousands of products and services that were supplied by Indiana and other states. As Michigan grew, so did the rest of the country. Indiana would have been very foolish if, in a fit of pique, it had decided not to buy Michigan's cheap cars or to require that Michigan buy as much from Indiana as it sold.

The analogy is not precise, but the message is identical. The envy and anger that many in the United States feel toward Japan's success should not blind policymakers to the reality that, as Japan (and every other nation of the world) grows richer, the United States will benefit. Just as it is easier for a company to prosper in a rapidly-growing market than to capture market share in a shrinking one, the United States will be more prosperous in a world in which knowledge, technology, and markets are proliferating, rather than one where the U.S. dominates a static or slowly-growing world economy.

Of course, if other nations grow much faster than the U.S. over a long period of time or if America loses its leadership in the most advanced technologies and the most rapidly-growing industries, the U.S. could become an economic also-ran, just as Britain and Argentina did previously. But the task of insuring continued strong U.S. growth has little to do with changing the behavior of the Japanese or the Koreans.

Instead, it involves changing in the propensity of Americans to borrow and spend rather than to save. This applies, not only to personal savings rates (Japanese households save about 16 percent of their incomes, compared to less than 5 percent for Americans) but more importantly to government borrowing and spending. It also involves major improvements in the educational preparation of large numbers of prospective workers (it has been observed that, in the competition between the U.S. and Japan, the world's best-educated lower half of the workforce is beating the world's best-educated upper half). And it involves reforming the incentives and institutions that encourage America's best and brightest to provide legal advice in corporate takeovers rather than to build companies that exploit new technologies.

Whatever is done to improve U.S. competitiveness must always be undertaken within the context of strengthening the world economy. It is in America's economic and political self-interest to restimulate the economies of the developing countries, where the fastest growth and productivity gains are still ahead. This may mean taking a much more aggressive role in leading multilateral efforts to rechannel excess savings from the trade surplus nations to the developing world. It also means trying to coordinate U.S. fiscal and monetary policies with other major nations, so that the world is pushed toward rapid growth rates near to those experienced during the 1950s and 1960s. And it means insuring that trade frictions do not lead to restrictions on trade in products, capital, or people, since these exchanges are the key to world dynamism and growth.

Improving Productivity in Service Industries

Manufacturing still controls the imagination, the statistics, and the policies of the nation, even though it no longer represents the most important activity in the American economy. The problem is most severe in the efforts that have been mounted to enhance the nation's productivity growth.

Most government steps to boost productivity have focused on such things as incentives for capital investment in industry, reduced environmental and antitrust regulation, retraining workers displaced from manufacturing plants, and preserving of the nation's industrial base against unfair foreign competition. The nation's mental image of progress is one in which American factories produce more cars, computers, and carpets per hour.

But these activities now represent a small and shrinking fraction of national employment and output. Moreover, manufacturing productivity performance has been relatively satisfactory and continues to improve.

Services are a far larger segment of the economy, where productivity has actually declined in recent years. These industries—health, education, trade, finance, insurance, real estate, and government—must be the targets of government efforts to improve productivity.

Two kinds of actions are needed:

• *Remove the Barriers to Competition in Services:* A huge portion of the service economy has not been touched by competition, ranging from education, which at the elementary and secondary level is a public monopoly, to health care, where control of costs has been in the hands of the providers. In the last decade, government has taken significant steps to deregulate transportation and communications, and competition in these fields has triggered major productivity gains.

Now the task is to bring competition to health, education, and government. While much of the responsibility rests with state and local officials, the federal government could provide powerful stimulus for change. For example, educational vouchers could serve to stimulate experimentation and competition in local schools. To make this competition effective, better measures of educational progress are needed—including standardized national tests that will enable schools, systems, and states to be compared with each other. Only when student learning progress is comprehensively assessed, and matched against investments of money and time, can productivity be judged. Without such measurable productivity data, there is no rational way to modify the system to attain higher standards and greater efficiency.

Competition in the schools should be mirrored in the health-care system. The steps that have been taken to reform Medicare and Medicaid to eliminate cost-plus reimbursement and institute fixed payments should be extended and perfected. Payment on a per person basis, greater emphasis on individual responsibility for health and for health-care costs, and rewards for efficient care providers should be implemented. These should be backed up with much more extensive monitoring of the results of treatment: comprehensive statistics on the effectiveness of various care and prevention strategies are needed if cost-effectiveness is to improve while quality is maintained. Productivity cannot be improved unless it can be systematically measured.

Beyond education and health care, many other services provided by government should be returned to the competitive economy. At the federal level, services ranging from air traffic control to the Post Office could be handled more productively by private contractors. At the state and local level, not only the traditionally private road-building and construction tasks, but sanitation, social services, corrections, transit, and many other services should be competitively bid.

In choosing to undertake the complex task of privatizing government services, it is important to focus on the long-term benefits of the strategy. Regardless of the calculus of immediate cost savings, (which are usually significant), the more important gains flow from the dynamism that private competition promotes. Competitors innovate. Bureaucracies respond—often slowly. Unless the government bureaucracies that now monopolize large segments of the economy are forced to compete, they will change slowly or not at all, and productivity will stagnate.

• *Invest in Technologies that Enhance Productivity in Services:* The federal government is one of the largest funders of research and development. Although most of these investments are in the defense and health industries, their impacts spread throughout the economy. For example, federal research funds have helped to underwrite the development of integrated circuits, computers, robots, and many other important technologies.

Little of the research that is funded by government is purposely aimed at improving the nation's productivity. And virtually none is directed to the important task of enhancing productivity in services.

But in two areas in particular, the government role is so overwhelming and the opportunities for productivity gains are so exciting that new R&D investments by the government should be considered. In education, for example, the potential for using integrated computer, video, and sound technologies to accelerate learning and improve the efficiency of the educational system is astounding. Although the development of hardware and software by private industry is proceeding, the risks are great, and the pace of progress and investment has been slow. If government were to invest in the development of a set of advanced, public-domain computerized courses for use in elementary, secondary, and postsecondary schools, the returns to the nation could well be spectacular in terms of learning gains, cost savings, and, in particular, the achievement of disadvantaged students. With the skills of the workforce an increasingly critical key to future economic success, such an investment by government—which would likely be less than $1 billion—could easily be justified.

In health care, the federal government currently spends $6 billion annually on health research. Yet, though the federal government pays more than $100 billion per year in health-care costs, few of its research dollars go to improve the efficiency of the industry. Instead, almost all federal research funds go toward advancing medical knowledge and developing new, often expensive, techniques for improving health and prolonging life. This strategy is the equivalent of General Motors spending all of its research funds on making bigger, fancier, faster cars and none on improving the efficiency of its factories.

While improved health is obviously a worthwhile social goal deserving government investment, ignoring research that could cut the cost of care threatens to undermine the objective of a healthier nation, by pricing health care out of reach. The potential for automation and other kinds of productivity-enhancing innovations in billing, diagnosis, testing, treatment, and care is enormous. Again, private industry is moving ahead in these fields, but there is substantial potential payoff from redirected government research spending.

Improving the Dynamism of an Aging Workforce

At the same time that the workforce is aging and becoming less willing to relocate, retrain, or change occupations, the economy is demanding more flexibility and dynamism. Despite general recognition of the importance of a flexible workforce, many national policies fail to promote this end.

For example, the nation's pension system is one in which most retirement benefits are tied to the job. In many cases, employees receive no benefits if they leave after a few years, and, by the time they reach mid-career, they will suffer major benefit losses if they switch employers. Designed primarily to insure company loyalty, the system now tends to inhibit workers from changing jobs and to discourage companies from hiring older workers. The federal government could encourage the restructuring of this inflexible system through changes in the tax code and other laws. For example, changes to encourage earlier vesting and greater portability, both of which would help to promote more flexibility by workers, could be encouraged with relatively modest changes in tax deductibility. IRAs, 401Ks, and similar savings-for-retirement plans could be enlarged and encouraged, rather than capped and discouraged as they were in recent tax changes.

Similarly, the unemployment insurance system has been largely used to provide income support to workers who are laid off. Relatively little has been done to make the system one that promotes relocation, retraining, and job search. Although the objective of encouraging workers to change may conflict with the humane goals of cushioning the impact of unemployment, from a national economic perspective, the system should be much more oriented toward stimulating movement and change by workers, rather than simply protecting them against joblessness.

For example, reforms that would require individuals to share in the cost of unemployment insurance (the equivalent of a deductible in other types of insurance) could help to discourage abuse of the system. Lump-sum payments for those who relocate or who return to work quickly could also encourage workers to make the difficult adjustments that may be necessary to find new jobs.

Although worker retraining has become a catchphrase, and the federal government and private industry now spend billions of dollars for retraining, there is still no national consensus that all workers should expect to learn new skills over the course of their worklives. Except in a few companies, training is confined mostly to managers and technical specialists, with little systematic effort to insure that all workers are constantly reinvesting in themselves to avoid obsolescence. National policies that promote such corporate and individual attitudes toward retraining should be backed up with changes in the tax code to encourage lifelong education.

For example, tax-favored individual training accounts that enable workers to save for their own reeducation should be tested. A program that allows students of all ages to borrow with federal guarantees (and uses the tax system to collect overdue accounts) deserves consideration. Because midlife, midcareer retraining faces so many personal, institutional, and financial obstacles, yet offers such significant payoffs to the national economy, a greater federal role is justified.

Finally, the goal of promoting dynamism requires reconsideration of national policies on immigration. The most careful studies of immigration have concluded that new entrants to the country not only do well in the labor market (without significantly hurting native workers), they soon become net contributors to the tax base and the national economy. The need for more, better-educated immigrants to help staff a growing economy will increase as the growth of the population and labor force slows in the 1990s.

At the same time that it is implementing a program to reduce illegal immigration, the nation should begin a program of gradually increasing its quotas for legal immigrants, opening its doors to more individuals desiring to enter the country. Beyond the apparent economic gains that such higher quotas will bring, immigration will provide important intangible benefits: entrepreneurial vitality, a more diverse national culture, a stronger sense of identification, and shared opportunities among the United States and the countries from which immigrants come.

Reconciling the Needs of Women, Work, and Families

America has become a society in which everyone is expected to work—including women with young children. This is a relatively recent trend. In 1960, only 11 percent of women with children under the age of six worked. Today 52 percent do. Because universal work is so new, the nation has not fully recognized the implications of the trend, much less adapted to it.

Many of society's institutions were designed during an era of male breadwinners and female homemakers. Some of these institutions, such as national leave policies, have perverse impacts, making it difficult for women to participate fully in the economy. Other policies and programs encourage some women (e.g., welfare mothers) to have children, while discouraging others from doing so (e.g., young couples with limited incomes).

The institutions and policies that govern the workplace should be reformed to allow women to participate fully in the economy and to insure that men and women have the time and resources needed to invest in their children. For example:

● *Time Off For Parents:* Working full-time and raising children demand more time, energy, and money than most parents have. While the challenge is great for a two-parent family with healthy children and enough money for day care, the problems can be overwhelming for a single parent with a limited income and a sick child.

The solution is straightforward, but expensive: more time away from work for parents. Flexible hours, the use of sick leave to care for children, more part-time work, pregnancy leaves for mothers and fathers, and other innovations offer parents time for child care. Seven of ten mothers would prefer part-time work, stay-at-home jobs, or flexible work hours, yet only half have such situations.

Short of mandating such changes as pregnancy leaves, the federal government might take steps to promote the use of part-time and flexible hours. For example, it could change the thresholds for Social Security and unemployment insurance taxes to make it less costly for employers to use part-time workers.

● *More High Quality Day Care:* When both parents work, the primary responsibility for child-raising falls to day care providers. The evidence shows that the quality of this care has large impacts on the subsequent success of the children.

Currently, only about 2000 of the nation's six million employers provide day care as a fringe benefit. Yet there is evidence that firms that provide day care assistance have less turnover, better success in recruiting employees, less absenteeism, and higher worker productivity than those that do not.

Over the next 13 years, it is likely that the most sophisticated employers will expand their support for day care. The government might assist and accelerate this trend by expanding the child care tax credit, creating a child care voucher, or by offering a tax credit to employers that assist with day care.

Other federal programs provide day care directly to poor children, notably Head Start. There is now persuasive evidence that early childhood education pays significant long-term social and economic dividends in terms of enhanced skills, better performance in school, increased employability, and reduced crime. More such investments in the care of poor children appear to be justified.

● *Welfare Reform:* The current welfare program was designed long before most women worked. Now that a majority of nonwelfare women with young children work, it no longer seems cruel to require welfare mothers to do so. The current system should be replaced with one that mandates work for all able-bodied mothers (excluding only those with infants), while providing training, day care, and job counseling. To be effective, the job requirement must be backed with a substantial job creation program at the state and local level.

Integrating Blacks and Hispanics Fully into the Workforce

For minority workers, the changes in the nation's demography and economy during the 1990s represent both a great risk and a great opportunity. With fewer new young workers entering the workforce, employers will be hungry for qualified people and more willing to offer jobs and training to those they have traditionally ignored. At the same time, however, the types of jobs being created by the economy will demand much higher levels of skill that the jobs that exist today. Minority workers are not only less likely to have had satisfactory schooling and on-the-job training, they may have language and attitude problems that prevent them from taking advantage of the jobs that will exist.

If the policies and employment patterns of the present continue, it is likely that the demographic opportunity of the 1990s will be missed and that, by the year 2000, the problems of minority unemployment, crime, and dependency will be worse than they are today. Without substantial adjustments, blacks and Hispanics will have a smaller fraction of the jobs of the year 2000 than they have today, while their share of those seeking work will have risen.

Each year of delay in seriously and successfully attacking this problem makes it more difficult. Not only will the jobs become more sophisticated and demanding, the numbers of new workers entering the workforce will begin to increase after 1993. Now is the time to renew the emphasis on education, training, and employment assistance for minorities that has been pursued with limited success over the past several decades. These investments will be needed, not only to insure that employers have a qualified workforce in the years after 2000, but finally to guarantee the equality of opportunity that has been America's great unfulfilled promise.

If new efforts to employ minority workers are to succeed where earlier efforts have failed, both individual attitudes and social institutions must change.

Traditional job training and employment programs by themselves are unlikely to have profound impacts on the future success of minority youth. Unless the $127 billion public educational system can somehow be better harnessed to serve minority youth, the $4 billion Job Training Partnership Act system can make only a small dent in the problem. For the public educational system to succeed with the minorities, however, may require radical changes. In school districts with the most serious problems, not only vouchers but complete privatization of the schools should be considered. Performance standards should be applied, not only to teachers but to students, administrators, and schools themselves. In practice, this might mean not only support for magnet schools that can be islands of excellence, but a willingness to close the worst schools, fire incompetent teachers, and expel disruptive students.

The complex interconnections between employment, education, literacy, cultural values, income, and living environments argue that employment problems cannot be solved without also addressing issues of individual and family responsibility. The choices are not simply between on-the-job training and basic skills remediation programs for teenagers, but among investments in child care, pregnancy prevention, welfare reform, big brother programs, and other possible interventions. Before minority unemployment can be significantly reduced, there must be change in the cultural values that make it seem more attractive to sell drugs or get pregnant than to do well in school and work at McDonald's.

Private employers have a new, and more expensive, role to play in the development of their workforces. Not only are they critically affected by the quality of the workers they will hire over the next 13 years, they are among the most knowledgeable designers and implementers of cost-effective, technology-based training programs. If there are real breakthroughs in training and hiring young disadvantaged workers between now and the year 2000, "second chance" educational systems developed at the worksite are likely to play a key role.

Improving Workers' Education and Skills

In previous centuries, the wealth of nations was thought to consist of gold in the national treasury and jewels in the emperor's crown. In more recent years, wealth has often been equated with factories, mines, and production machinery within a nation's borders.

As the miraculous rebirth of Europe and Japan after World War II has proven, however, the foundation of national wealth is really people—the human capital represented by their knowledge, skills, organizations, and motivations. Just as the primary assets of a modern corporation leave the workplace each night to go home for dinner, so the income-generating assets of a nation are the knowledge and skills of its workers—not its industrial plants or natural resources.

As the economies of developed nations move further into the post-industrial era, human capital plays an ever more important role in their progress. As the society becomes more complex, the amount of education and knowledge needed to make a productive contribution to the economy becomes greater. A century ago, a high school education was thought to be superfluous for factory workers and a college degree was the mark of an academic or a lawyer. Between now and the year 2000, for the first time in history, a majority of all new jobs will require postsecondary education. Many professions will require nearly a decade of study following high school, and even the least skilled jobs will require a command of reading, computing, and thinking that was once necessary only for the professions.

Education and training are the primary systems by which the human capital of a nation is preserved and increased. The speed and efficiency with which these education systems transmit knowledge govern the rate at which human capital can be developed. Even more than such closely-watched indicators as the rate of investment in plant and equipment, human capital formation plays a direct role in how fast the economy can grow.

If every child who reaches the age of seventeen between now and the year 2000 could read sophisticated materials, write clearly, speak articulately, and solve complex problems requiring algebra and statistics, the American economy could easily approach or exceed the 4 percent growth of the boom scenario. Unconstrained by shortages of competent, well-educated workers, American industry would be able to expand and develop as rapidly as world markets would allow. Boosted by the productivity of well-qualified workforce, U.S.-based companies would reassert historic American leadership in old and new industries, and American workers would enjoy the rising standards of living they enjoyed in the 1950s and 1960s.

If this bright future is to be realized, the educational standards that have been established in the nation's schools must be raised dramatically. Put simply, students must go to school longer, study more, and pass more difficult tests covering more advanced subject matter. There is no excuse for vocational programs that "warehouse" students who perform poorly in academic subjects or for diplomas that register nothing more than years of school attendance. From an economic standpoint, higher standards in the schools are the equivalent of competitiveness internationally.

Promoting world growth, boosting service industry productivity, stimulating a more flexible workforce, providing for the needs of working families with children, bringing minority workers into the workforce, and improving the educational preparation of workers are not the only items on the nation's agenda between now and the year 2000. But they are certainly among the most important.

More critically, they are issues that will not go away by themselves. If nothing unusual is done to focus national attention and action on these challenges, they are likely still to be with the nation at the beginning of the next century. By addressing them now, the nation's decisionmakers can help to assure that the economy and the workforce fulfil their potential to make the year 2000 the beginning of the next American century.